FIX THAT SHIT

A COUPLES GUIDE TO GETTING
PAST THE STICKY STUFF

BY

CHANTAL HEIDE

Chantal Heide
www.canadasdatingcoach.com

Ordering Information:
Quantity sales. Special discounts are available on quantity purchases by corporations, associations, and others. For details, contact the publisher at the address above.

Printed in Canada
Chantal Heide.
Fix That Shit – A Couples Guide To Getting Past The Sticky Stuff / Chantal Heide

p. cm.

ISBN 13 - 978-1540898531
ISBN 10 - 1540898539

1. Family and Relationships —Dating

Second Edition
14 13 12 11 10 / 10 9 8 7 6 5 4 3 2 1

Other books by Chantal Heide

Comeback Queen – Make A Triumphant Return To Dating After Divorce

Fake Love Need Not Apply – The Single Girls Guide To Avoiding Posers Losers Scammers And Predators Online

No More Assholes – Your 7 Step Guide to Saying Goodbye to Guys and Finding the Real Man You're Looking For

After The First Kiss – 7 Steps That Make Your First Year Together Ridiculously Awesome

Say Yes To Goodness – 10 Steps To A Complete And Happy You

For Dennis Heide

Content

Acknowledgements

I wouldn't be this happy without the loving support of people who gave me space to grow.

I'd like to thank my husband for his tenacity and devotion, without him I wouldn't be the person I am today. Or I might have been. Who knows, but here we are now and I'm grateful for his love and courage.

As always, I'm grateful to Kit Duncan for her incredible editing skills, firm hand on my back, and LOL moments every time we work together.

Thank you to my mom and dad for always loving and supporting me. It's a crazy ride sometimes, but they're still beside me every step of the way.

And of course thank you to my strong tribe of girlfriends and my wonderful fur babies, without whom life would lack balance.

And thank you, my fans. Together we're going to make the world a better place, filled with love, support, and understanding.

Let's do this!

Foreword

Iunderstand if you're reading this book and wondering: How can I change him so we can have a better relationship? We're taught to look outside ourselves for what's going to bring happiness and satisfaction, and if we can mould the outer world just a little better everything is going to start going our way.

If I complain enough maybe he'll change. If I let this issue go today maybe we'll have a better conversation about it tomorrow. If I freeze out my words and affection maybe he'll realize just how much he needs to make me happier. If I'm uncooperative maybe he'll understand how unhappy I really am.

I want to prepare you for what's actually in this book – a manual on how to affect other people's behaviours by altering your own. See, we have a tendency to overlook the effect even our smallest gestures have while maintaining a hyper-focus on how much other people's behaviours are affecting our sense of well-being.

But how empowered are you feeling? How happy are you today? Are you frustrated by the fact that no matter what you try nothing is changing, and every day you find yourself spinning round the same issues in your relationship? Are you at the end of your rope, tired of conversations that you hoped would fix problems ending up in the pile of talks that resolved absolutely nothing?

Well, guess what? You're basically normal. In today's culture resolutions are few and far between, primarily because real solutions don't make it into mainstream media. How many times do you see someone learn how to calm their own emotions through meditation and practice kindness first in order to turn the tides in their love life? How often are women talking about how fixing themselves fixed everything?

We've developed a culture that thrives on anger and frustration, and I don't discount for a second how those emotions can make you feel alive. But there's another way, and it's easy and fun and peaceful and life changing, and this new method makes it oh so easy to achieve and maintain real change and growth in every aspect of your life.

Yes, it takes work on your part. Yes, it takes focus and consistency. Yes, it's all about you and only you. And it's not about blaming yourself for what you do and don't do, it's about putting the power of change squarely in the hands of the only person who can truly affect your life. You.

You, my love, carry the sword to point up at the sky, beckoning the powers that be to fill you with the strength and stamina to go out there and knock bull crap right out of the ballpark.

You are capable of changing your thought patterns and getting out of that incessant spin mode.

You have the ability to calm your emotions and enjoy a more satisfying union.

And once you read this book, you'll have to tools to affect the change you want in your relationships.

Because life begins when you ask the right question. So let's switch tracks, from "how can I get him to change" to "what can I do to change what's happening around me." This is where the true power lies: right in the palm of your hand.

Step 1 – Grounding

All things being equal, the simplest solution tends to be the best one.

~ William of Ockham

CHAPTER 1

Fix That Shit

I stared moodily out the car window, watching the lush West Virginia landscape whirl by as we drove south to our springtime rock climbing destination. *What the heck had just happened?* I thought, my mind racing back and forth, trying to pin down the reason why we'd started fighting in the first place.

My first husband Mike drove silently, waves of frustration emanating from his tense posture and pursed lips. We'd stopped fighting only because we'd stopped talking, but the discontent still lay heavily in the air between us. I hated these moments.

It had been a stupid argument over a stupid topic, the kind that doesn't even need a description because the pattern was more relevant than the reasoning. A difference of opinions, a passionate flare up over who was wrong, a sharp word, a stinging retort. Then, pissed off silence.

We used silence as a defense against getting angrier, but our irate feelings continued to boil under the surface.

Now what?

I turned my attention away from spinning over how much of a dick I thought he was and backtracked to the beginning of our conversation, looking for clues. I wanted to find out what had triggered the whole thing so I could feel justified, validated, and in essence, right.

And then my stomach growled.

Fourteen years ago the word "hangry" wasn't in our collective vocabulary, but it suddenly dawned on me that we had gotten up before the crack of dawn to tackle the nine hour drive to New River Gorge, rushing to arrive with enough time to settle in and scope out some climbs before the day's end. I was tired, I was hungry, and I was grumpy as hell.

"Bumby," I said gently, the angry tornado in my mind losing steam, no longer whipping my thoughts into a frenzy. "I'm hungry, and it's making me crabby. I'm sorry about that. Let's stop for something to eat."

He looked at me, a glint of humour in his eye.

"Fix that shit," he retorted, and we laughed.

Fix that shit. That statement became our new go to phrase whenever one of us confessed to inadvertently starting a battle over misinterpreted and misdirected emotions.

You're coming home in a bad mood because you keep having conflicts with your boss? Fix that shit.

You're feeling hormonal and find yourself rampaging? Fix that shit.

You didn't sleep well last night, had a stressful day work, didn't eat enough, and now you're crashing and lashing out…

Fix that shit.

How simple.

CHAPTER 2

Worry About Yourself

You're stressed out. You go to bed worrying about what you're not resolving, you're waking up wondering what's going to happen today, and you're spending your days having conversations in your head with your partner, trying to find the words that'll get your relationship through this rough patch once and for all.

One day drags into another, spinning round and round the same issues, and you don't see the light at the end of the tunnel.

You've tried counselling, maybe separately, maybe together, maybe both. You've read books, googled articles, vented to friends, cried quietly in the bathroom. You're hurt, you're angry, you're frustrated, and you're just plain tired of wondering how you'll ever get back to feeling close again.

But you're not willing to give up.

You know that deep down, under this dark cloud of emotional discomfort, lies a great relationship. You share the same values, you make each other laugh when you're not making each other miserable, and the sight of him still makes your heart skip, even if sometimes you hate him a little or a lot.

He's a good father, a hardworking man, his integrity is commendable and his desire to be a positive force for those he cares for is something you deeply admire about him. His faults and flaws are outweighed by his character and strength, and you still love him.

And you know, despite the fights you have, he still loves you.

Your relationship has become a battleground because neither of you is willing to throw in the towel and give up. You're both feeling the pain that comes with wanting to live the loving relationship you feel deep down but can't because the anger, angst, and frustration buzzing between you keeps interfering with the underlying harmony of your love.

It could be so good, you keep thinking.

I often say, "Life begins when you ask the right question," because only when you set your mind on the right course will you get to where you really want to go. A scientific approach to any problem begins with the question that needs answering, and if you're going to be effective in tackling your relationship issues you have to start with the question that's going to help you reach your goal.

"What will I say to him tonight?"

"When should I bring this up? How?"

"Are we ever going to resolve this?"

"Will we be better able to talk about this if I let the topic settle for a week or two before bringing it up again?"

Questions like these can go through your mind on a daily basis, but you're wondering how to approach the airport runway without asking yourself if the landing gear is down.

How emotionally ready are you to let go of the negative feelings that have been bandied back and forth between you? If you fix this problem today will you be calm tomorrow, or will something else take its place?

Because here's the thing: There's a huge possibility that despite your deep desire to get past the issues in your relationship your brain isn't prepared to do so. You might fix this particular fight today, but if the wiring in your head isn't properly set you'll revert to the same patterns tomorrow.

Fighting, anger, and frustration will creep back into your relationship because putting electrical tape on cracked and fraying wires doesn't fix anything. You need to pull the whole thing out and put fresh wires in, plugging them into the right spots so the sparks don't ever fly again.

Is that possible? Yes. But only when you start with the right question in mind.

That question isn't "How can I get him to change?" or even "How can I fix these fights?" That last one, however, is a great question to have at the back of your mind.

No, the most important question right now should be, "How can I settle my mind?"

You see, you can't change what he thinks, how he feels, or any of his reactions. Trying to find a solution with those ideas in mind is a distraction from what you actually have the power to affect at this very moment, and that's you.

The biggest mistake you'll make in a relationship is under valuing the effects your gestures have. But with the advice in this book you'll be able to affect major changes not only towards each other, but also how he thinks, feels, and behaves, simply by turning your focus back onto yourself.

Oh my God, you think, *If he feels like I'm not even bothering to work on us he's going to think I'm totally selfish and tapping out!*

It's more likely he'll feel relieved to have some pressure taken off him for a while. If he's aware of just how much your thought process is fixated on him and his reactions or contributions to issues, he's feeling the weight of your gaze every day and wondering where the next landmine lies.

Whenever I talk about a solution to a problem I always say now is the time to try something different. So if you think about how long your attention has been ping ponging back and forth between your feelings and his, your reactions and his, and maybe most of all, what he's doing wrong to contribute to all this upheaval, giving him a break while you sit down for a minute to come up with another plan is going to feel like a reprieve from all the contention.

The fact is, if your relationship has become a battleground with both sides battling to the point of exhaustion it's time to call back the troops, sit down with the generals, and come up with a whole new plan of attack. And I'm all for transparency in a relationship, so go ahead and let him know what you're doing. Tell him, "I love you, and I hate all this disagreeing we've been doing. I'm going to take a break from it and do some things that are going to slow my mind down and make my brain feel more peaceful."

If he asks what you're doing, show him the exercises in this book. He might be curious, or he might simply be happy hearing that you're shifting your focus. But don't worry if he's not looking to do all the calming things you're going to learn here. If there's one thing I've learned, it's that it only takes one leader to change the whole thing around.

You see, I've been where you are in my own relationship. My hubby and I spent almost nine years either fighting about something or being quiet in a desperate attempt to not fill every minute trying to work out the stewing in our minds. So even when we weren't fighting (or as I like to call it, having a heated negotiation) we were still feeling hugely unsettled. It was hard, and it felt shitty.

But I turned it all around when I learned how to deal with my own brain. Did it still take time for the dust to settle once I'd mastered myself? It did, and that's the definition of leading. Leading means "I'm going to go first, and you're free to follow." It took about a year, from the time I took control of myself and put all my focus on what I was doing to feel better to where we are today, which is 100% fight free for nearly two years (so long as we don't talk about American politics).

We're no different from anyone else either. We're two normal people with strong opinions coming into a relationship with dysfunction and baggage stemming from our histories, and we both stumble through this world trying our best to not hurt the people we care for.

But neither of us had a manual on how to love and communicate. Our parents never sat us down and taught us how to effectively resolve conflicts while making sure our brains didn't go crazy on us. There were no Relationship 101 classes in school to go with our Sex Ed, and I don't remember any books in the school library about how to make sure our adult relationships didn't end up hanging by a thread.

Like the majority of couples we were walking around in the dark without a flashlight and tripping over the emotional suitcases scattered around.

We were lost, but I found the way, and it only takes one person to turn on the lights, clear the path, read the manual, and do the exercises to fix the problems and create something amazing in a relationship. But it all starts with a hero. You.

And it's normal to start with you. Why? Let me ask you this – who's more likely to go to counselling, men or women? Who's more likely to pick up a self-help book at the store or sit and talk for hours about issues in their relationships, work, and lives with their peers?

Women.

In fact, a British study done between 2012 and 2013 found that 62% of the people who asked to be referred for counselling for anxiety or depression were women (1). Does that mean men are less emotional and therefore less prone to suffering from emotional issues?

Nope.

Here's another factoid about men – they're equally, if not more, emotional than women. There's this great research center in Brighton, England called MindLab that's all about decoding human emotions. They do a lot of work for media and government agencies, and they're awesome at divulging what makes us tick.

MindLab conducted a study in which they hooked men and women up to machines that measured heart rates, body temperatures, respiration rates, brain waves and even changes in pupil dilation to track responses and get insight into emotional reactions while viewing images that were either funny, exciting, blissful, or heartwarming (2).

They found that men were similar to us when it came to funny, exciting and blissful, yet their responses skyrocketed to twice ours when it came to heartwarming.

But.

When asked about their emotional responses after the test, 67% admitted to under-reporting how they'd felt.

Conclusion? Men have feelings too, but they hate to admit it.

So it falls on us to be the emotional leader in relationships because we're more adapted to reflecting, analyzing, and discussing what happens in our heads and hearts. It's just something we do.

Do men welcome us as emotional leaders? I'll answer this one based entirely on my personal experience and from what I've observed in my practice. Yes!

They respond so well to what we model that I can't help but realize the best remedy for upheavals in relationships is how we carry ourselves emotionally.

Will the advice in this book work for every relationship? If you've committed to a man and not a guy, you have a huge chance for success. I have yet to see a man not change his behaviours once the woman he cares for implements my advice.

But again, it all starts with taking your eyes off him and turning your focus inward. Taking responsibility for yourself is key here, and as far as I'm concerned nothing will change until you do.

So if you're ready to work on you, then you're ready for some amazing transformations in your love life.

Ready? Let's do it!

CHAPTER 3

Put Your Oxygen Mask on First

If you've ever taken a flight you know exactly what I'm talking about. Before a plane takes off flight attendants are busy elegantly pointing out the exits here, here, and there, and if the oxygen masks drop down from the ceiling you need to strap your own on before helping the kiddo beside you. Why? Because in a situation where a cabin is depressurized and the air is quickly depleted you have mere seconds before your oxygen starved brain stops functioning properly.

Which means if you're struggling to put theirs on first, both of you might pass out before you succeed.

Now look at your relationship. It might have taken off smoothly, but somewhere along the way some heavy turbulence started shaking things up, and now's the time to strap on that oxygen mask and make sure your brain is going to stay lucid enough for you to help those you love.

Because let's face it, unless your brain is functioning properly you're pretty much useless to anybody else.

Which is why I want to start with your head. Getting your brain to work properly is the first step towards having a healthy relationship, and skipping this step is like discarding the oxygen tank before going scuba diving. Ya ain't gonna get far.

What I'm saying is, fixing your brain will breathe new life into your relationship.

Getting tired of the oxygen analogies yet? I'm hoping I'm making enough to stress the importance of not skipping the instructions in this first step, because without the calming exercises I'm going to teach you you're just going to keep gasping for air.

Okay, enough said. Let's start.

First, I want you to understand your brain. You might have rarely given thought to that particular organ and how it functions, but you need to know that you have much more control over it than you realize. See, there's a phenomenon we're hearing more and more about called neuroplasticity, and it's exactly what you think. Your brain is supple and mouldable just like plasticine is, and it's literally putty in your hands.

But if you're not the one shaping it it's getting pushed this way and that by other hands, and as a result you feel like there's a foreign object inside your skull doing things you're really not enjoying, like triggering nasty emotional outcomes and spinning roller coaster rides through hell.

The upside is you can take control at any time and start shaping your brain into something that works for you instead of against you. And it's not even hard at all. In fact, once you start taking control you quickly get addicted to how easy it is and how great it feels.

Easy? Great? Yup. So let's start.

CHAPTER 4

This is Your Brain on Meditation

Your brain loves meditation. It's like (insert most soothing thing you can possibly imagine here). It's natural for your brain to rest and relax on a regular basis, to not be constantly bombarded with images and words and sounds and be able to just lull itself into a quiet space.

I want you to take a moment to transport yourself to the life your ancestors lived a few hundred thousand years ago. Our predecessors, early Homo sapiens, experienced short, danger filled lives, but they also lived in times where they cohabited in close, tribal groups surrounded by nature. Sure, they had a lot of moments where they were fearful, but their hunting-gathering existence meant they also zoned out picking berries, digging up roots, quietly hunting, tanning skins, roaming beautiful territories, and peacefully working together to ensure the survival of the group.

Repetitive, quiet, monotonous exercises were a perfect balance to those moments when their fight or flight responses put them on high alert, flooding their systems with high doses of cortisol (their stress hormone) and adrenaline (the shot in the arm that boosted strength and speed). These sedative activities kept them balanced and grounded.

But what are we doing today to counter all those occasions where our brains are triggered into fight or flight mode? You know, the heart stopping moment when the jerk in the BMW cuts you off, that spike in anxiety when you get to work and find out pink slips were being handed out, getting stuck in traffic on the way home, being late driving Sophie to baseball practice, and fighting with your partner about this and that? Not to mention topping all that off with media bent on triggering our emotional responses with a bombardment of images designed to ignite our fear responses.

When one thing after another seems to go wrong and even taking a vacation doesn't have the relaxing effect you were hoping for, it's time to start getting pro-active in giving your mind the break it needs.

Because here's the thing: Your brain can start taking on a mind of its own. Like a parrot it's going to start mimicking the very things it's exposed to the most, and if you don't want it to start screeching "Dammit!" over and over you better start paying attention to what you're exposing it to. If you never take a moment to consciously interrupt the flow of anxiety all you're going to feel is stress and anxiety.

But if you interrupt that process and redirect your brain into calm, peaceful spots you'll find that with time it'll get easier and easier to not only let go of negative feelings, but eventually avoid them almost completely no matter what's going on around you.

This means no longer being susceptible to other people's moods or getting angry and frustrated when maneuvering through dense traffic. It means maintaining a sense of serenity when your boss is on the rampage, and being able to stay calm and loving when your loved ones are lashing out because they can't explain their own unsettled feelings without looking for a scapegoat.

But more than that, it means waking up in the morning with a heightened sense of contentment after a good night's sleep. Yes, I said a good night's sleep, because you'll notice a heightened quality in your sleep too.

It means smiling more at the checkout counter, being more benevolent when someone wants to enter your lane on the roads, and feeling like all those little BS moments other people are reacting to really just don't matter.

Basically, it means not getting caught up in the negativity the world around you constantly spews while feeling like you yourself are a source of light and love. And because ultimately like attracts like, it means drawing out the same qualities from those around you while shedding the people who refuse to practice peacefulness.

Sweet. Right?

Think for a second about what you really want to be surrounded by day in and day out. What are you seeking in your life, emotionally and mentally? Security, peace, contentment, joy, love, optimism... I could go on and on. None of us, in a sane state of mind, are seeking to fill our lives with unrest, anger, sadness, or discomfort. The beauty of meditation is the change that takes place not only in your brain but in your psyche over all as the toll of negative emotions are diminished and replaced by the benefits of positive emotions.

Your brain on meditation is not only changed in regards to how it functions and reacts, it changes how your body reacts and how those around you react. Your inner and outer worlds morph into something that starts to work with you and for you instead of against you. Anxiety goes down, as do stress and fatigue. Patience levels go up, along with compassion and forgiveness. Understanding and your ability to not internalize other people's angst rise, and your loved ones are drawn closer to you as a result.

You'll see, but only when you give yourself a chance to experience the gains a few minutes of quieting your brain will give you.

CHAPTER 5

Harvard Says

If you're still on the fence about what meditation can do for you, then take a moment to listen to what Harvard says happens to your brain when you make calming your mind a regular part of your schedule.

I've said you won't have a new life with the same brain, and it's true. If you want to create a 180 in your life and relationships you need to change the brain that got you here in the first place. Otherwise, it's like showing up for a job interview in jogging pants and spaghetti stains on your shirt. By some grace of God you might get what you're looking for, but it's going to be a mighty steep uphill battle.

But changing the physical make-up of your brain puts you in the right headspace to get everything right. How? Why? Because the areas affected by meditation, the areas that actually physically morph and change shape, are the areas you most need to deal with in order to create the new you.

MRI brain scans taken by Harvard before and after participants meditated on average of 27 minutes a day for 8 weeks showed that the human brain goes through some remarkable transformations. Bad parts shrank, and good parts got bigger.

Let's start with the bad part.

Your amygdala, also known as the fight or flight center buried deep in the oldest part of your brain, is what triggers a burst of adrenaline and cortisol when you have a fear response. When you get into a fight and your heart rate goes up and your muscles get tense, that's your amygdala preparing you for either a battle royale or a run for the hills.

Fear is a huge contributor to fights, especially fear of the unknown. Is this going to be the fight that ends our relationship? What will I do if I lose my partner? Is he lying to me about something? Am I doing the right thing?

All these fearful thoughts are either byproducts or contributors to your amygdala shooting off, and they're having a terrible effect on your system. Never mind the damaging repercussions that high levels of stress and their associated increased levels of cortisol have on your thyroid, immune system, muscles, bones, and connective tissues (3). Never mind how repeated high levels of adrenaline will shrink your hippocampus, affecting your memory and ability to feel compassion while inhibiting your ability to create new neural pathways in that area of your brain (4). All those are bad enough, but what you're truly aware of when your amygdala is too big is how you feel.

Stressed and shitty.

You have difficulty feeling calm and settled. You have difficulty overcoming negative feelings like anxiety, and worst of all, you have a hard time feeling good about yourself or the world in general. It's a horrible tailspin into depression and angst.

And look at how that's affecting your outer world. Your heightened anxiety has you constantly on the lookout for where the next battle will come from, poised and ready to either defend yourself or attack. Being unable to see yourself in as positive a light as you should gives you feelings of inadequacy and insecurity, and the melting pot of those negative feelings keep dragging you deeper and deeper into a dark pit of emotional distress.

You don't want this. Your loved ones don't want you to suffer this, and they certainly don't want to suffer because you're suffering. You know the saying, *When mamma ain't happy, ain't nobody happy?* Well, we're going to fix that whole cycle by reducing the size of your amygdala. If it sounds too simple, then maybe it's time to release the notion that only complicated answers could be the right ones. Remember, sometimes a lifeline is nothing more than a floating donut on a rope.

Now let's look at the other part of your brain that's affected by meditation, your hippocampus (5). This region of your brain actually grows during meditation and is the area responsible for your memory retention, introspection, compassion, and drives not only how you feel about others but about yourself as well.

Feel like you're suffering from low self-esteem? Then it's time to grow your hippocampus and reverse the effect of cortisol and adrenaline your amygdala has been dumping on your thoughts and feelings. Finding that you're hyper focused on everything your loved ones are doing wrong and having a hard time remembering what they've done right? Time to grow your hippocampus.

And how are you feeling about your own actions? Are you constantly beating yourself up because no matter which way you turn you can't seem to do the right thing? Then let's get that hippocampus developing so you start to recognize just how awesome you really are.

If all this sounds complicated, it's not. It's no harder than sitting in a chair on a regular basis. You're already doing that, right? Same thing, except what you're changing is what you're doing while in that chair.

Let me teach you the five steps that makes it all so simple to do.

CHAPTER 6

The 5 Steps to Blissing Out

" Meditation is hard, isn't it? Don't you have to stop thinking for a long time?"

No, and no. Keep in mind that it takes a fraction of a second for your brain to know it's doing something different and change in response to that difference. People tend to have a lot of anxiety about meditation, thinking that unless they're Zenning like the white robed Guru on the mountain they're achieving nothing, and because of that they avoid starting altogether. That's just plain wrong.

The fact is your brain is an amazing piece of machinery and the slightest modification still has an effect. So if you're getting in 10 seconds of blank mind space during a 20 minute session you're changing your brain, literally one split second at a time.

The second most common question I get about meditation is, "How do you do it?" Again, easy peasy, no contorting your legs into uncomfortable positions while sitting on pillows in flowing robes necessary. Just find a spot to sit and close your eyes, and you've accomplished a big part of the task.

To make it even easier, I've broken it down to 5 steps you'll want to remember each time.

1 – Sit up straight. You don't want to end up with a sore back when you're done, so grab a cushion and put it between you and the backrest if you need some extra help getting your spine straight. Being comfortable is an important part of meditation! So avoid getting a kink in your neck by keeping your head straight, and avoid strained shoulders and lower back pain by aligning your spine.

2 – Relax your body. It's important to bring your focus to your body and ensure you're relaxing any tense spots. We tend to unconsciously tighten up as a defensive reflex, and now is a good time to touch base with your physical body and unwind some of those muscles. Bring your focus to each area at a time and relax any tightness you feel. Keep cycling through all the individual parts of your body throughout the time you're sitting in meditation. Even after all these years I have to keep relaxing parts that tense up during my sessions.

3 – Bring your focus back. Let's face it, part of being a woman means our minds are running all day long. In fact, compared to men we need 20 more minutes of sleep a night to compensate for all that mental multitasking we do. You'll find yourself compiling lists or interior decorating while trying to meditate, and that's okay. It's normal because it's what your brain is used to doing, running off on tangents. Don't worry about how many times you realize you're off in thought because it's not how many times you're thinking that matters, it's how many times you bring your focus back. Remember, even a second has an impact.

Pretend you're looking at the spot right in front of your face, about an inch from the bridge of your nose. This is the space where here and now resides, and that's exactly where you want to be. Here is where your physical body is sitting in this chair. Now is this very moment where nothing is happening except for you sitting in this chair. Focus on that. Let yourself become drawn entirely right here, feel your focus get drawn into your brain and flow with the sounds filling it, whether it's the sound of your breathing or the music you've picked out.

4 – Breathe. Don't worry about becoming a master breather when you start. Keep it simple, and go for what's slow and deep and comfortable for you. Bringing your focus back using your breath as a focal point is a great technique. Just remember to keep it comfortable and not stress about whether or not you're breathing slow or deep enough. If it's more relaxed than how you normally do it you're on the right track.

5 – Surrender. This is the best part. I use the words "I surrender" as my mantra when I sit down to meditate, and it helps me get into that relaxed space much easier. Just keep mentally repeating "I surrender" over and over, letting those words replace anything else you think about. You're surrendering thinking, worrying, fixing, and feeling. This is the phrase that allows you to flow from your current state of stress and anxiety to one where you feel more relaxed and in control. You're giving up your present state of mind and yielding to another, and it's this surrender that's going to help unclench your brain.

Words have a powerful impact on our lives. You're well aware that a kind word can lift your spirits while hurtful ones resonate even after they've been said, twisting and turning in your mind for far too long. One of the things I'm going to teach you is how to use words to your advantage, and it all starts here, with these two.

The words "I surrender" don't mean you give up, and they don't mean you've been weakened. These two words mean you're ready to stop fighting all your inner and outer demons. They are the beginning of peace, the end to war, the first step to reconciliation with the new you. "I surrender" is the most powerful thing you can do in this moment of your life, putting yourself in charge of your evolution.

You've been dangling around like a puppet on a string, being jerked about by your over active amygdala and under active hippocampus for long enough, and you're done fighting the effects this war has had on your emotions. I surrender!

CHAPTER 7

Why Surrender Makes You Strong

I've worked with so many women who shudder at the thought of putting down their swords and shields, and you know what? I've been one of them. The thought of letting my man see tears in my eyes was unacceptable. See me weak? Not on your life. See me vulnerable? No way, José. I am strong. I am impenetrable. I will stand firmly by my convictions while hiding my feelings until you see how right I am and meet me on the other side of this emotional wall.

But let me paint a picture for you. Every time you hide your true feelings you're turning the sword on yourself, and slowly but surely you and your relationship are coming closer and closer to dying a death from a thousand cuts. Individually, none of those shallow slices will kill you, but because each one draws blood eventually you're going to be drained dry, and there'll be nothing left but a pale, crumbled mess on the floor.

When I finally decided to stop holding back my true feelings do you know what my husband said to me? "I had no idea you felt this way." And things started to change because finally he was seeing how affected I was by the things that hurt me. As for me, I started to cycle though my feelings instead of staying stuck in them, and releasing them became liberating.

Discard the notion that bringing forth your feelings and laying them out makes you weak. We picked up that idea somewhere in our past, maybe from our parents or maybe from TV and movies, but it's got to go. If you've never heard the saying "The truth will set you free," let me bring it to light for you now. In order for you and your relationship to be truly real you have to allow yourself to be real. Only then will you heal not only yourself, but any rifts that have developed in your love life.

Because here's the thing: You and your partner want to love each other fully, deeply, and honestly. Letting yourself accept and release your emotions into this union allows him to love all of you, and it allows you to love him for accepting you. This is what true intimacy is all about.

"But I'll be a hot mess!" Well, yes and no. Let me introduce you to Phase 2 of your meditation routine.

CHAPTER 8

Being Appropriately Emotional

Let's be honest here. If you've become a pro at stuffing down your feelings chances are you've got a lot bubbling under the surface. Sometimes what you're emotional about is a little bit about what just happened and a lot about backed up feelings trying to push their way out.

It's time to let all those long awaiting emotions free, because doing so will place both feet more firmly in your current, emotional reality. So let's start unleashing what's not rooted in your relationship, those things that happened before you got together that you didn't dare unearth so they can stop haunting your relationship like a bully poltergeist.

How? In a functional, healing manner, one that allows you to fully delve into your feelings without restraint, embarrassment, or the kind of time constraints we put on ourselves when we start to cry in front of people. Let's give you a chance to purge the old so there's room for something newer and better.

This is something I had to learn the hard way. See, I was super strong and stoic, traits I learned to develop in my childhood and subsequently brought into my relationships. See me cry? Nope. My poor relationship choices didn't get to see they affected me that deeply. Add the trauma of losing a sibling at 17, something I'd never learned to work through, and I had a lot of rotted emotional stuffing filling up every last bit of me.

I had a lot of anger, grief, sadness, and anxiety boiling under my calm exterior, and I thought getting through life functionally meant doing my best to put those feelings on a back burner. But back burner stuff doesn't go away. It boils and boils, and if you don't watch out it boils over and makes a mess all over your stove. Then you've gotta lift up the front burner stuff and clean up the mess underneath, and it all starts feeling frustrating, tedious, and complicated.

So, here's how you release your old emotions and stop messes from happening.

Get into the habit of meditating, because soon enough you're going to fall in love with it. There's something that happens when your brain waves change that I call "the sweet spot." This is the place where the real magic happens. It's hard to describe, but when you've been there you know exactly what I'm talking about. It's a shift that takes place inside your head as your brainwave frequency changes from its regular daytime functioning rhythm to a deeper state. Technically, from Beta waves to either Alpha or Theta.

This altered state is the perfect place to upheave those old emotions because what you'll experience is a release of their physical effect while your brain is relaxed, meaning they'll leave your body without upsetting your mind. It's so cathartic.

You know as well as I do how *physical* emotions are. Fear squeezes your lungs, anxiety boils in your stomach, and sadness chokes up your throat. But every time you repress one of those emotions you store it somewhere deep inside of you, and ultimately all those caged feelings start to make you sick, either mentally or physically or both.

It's time to let all those physical reactions take place. You'd have to do it eventually, and either they're going to come out in a spewing vomit on the people who triggered them or you can let them out when you decide to let them run their course. It's your choice, but trust me when I say you're going to love controlling their release. You think you were in control when you held them back? Nope. The true definition of control is being capable of letting them go on your own terms.

So get into that chair you love to meditate in, put on your headphones and choose your favourite relaxing track on my YouTube channel. Relax, surrender, and get into your sweet spot. Once you're there ask yourself this question:

How am I feeling?

When I first started meditating I thought the whole point was getting on top of the feelings of anxiety that would well up, to just ignore and push down any emotions that tried to interfere with the calm I was attempting to create during meditation. But with time it got harder and harder until finally one day I just said "Fuck it!" and went with it. And do you know what? That's how I finally learned exactly how to deal with my feelings. By embracing them.

Finally, I surrendered to what was trying to escape all along. All those negative feelings weren't going anywhere, and my denial wasn't doing anything to alleviate them. There's a quote from Bill Hicks, a sadly departed stand-up comic whose brilliance equalled George Carlin, that says it best: "Your denial is beneath you, and thanks to the use of hallucinogenic drugs, I see through you."

Your denial of your feelings aren't something you created. It's a stigma that you accepted, but you're better than that. You're stronger than that. You're meant to be a whole human being, with feelings and upswings and yes, even downswings. This crazy roller coaster ride is ultimately a lesson in appreciation for all that you can experience, but denying the entirety of the human condition makes you miserable because it's counter to what you're supposed to do. Quit that. Seriously. Be human; it's beautiful and tragic and amazing and sad, and there's so much to learn from it all.

When you reside in your sweet spot and ask "How am I feeling?" something happens inside you. A gate opens and you feel physical sensations begin to materialize inside your body. This is the physiological responses of your supressed feelings, and this is what you need to release so they don't affect your mental or physical health or the health of your relationships.

They're going to feel uncomfortable, as negative feelings tend to do. But because you're doing this on your time, on your terms, you can now comfortably allow them to materialize and fully run their course.

Here are 5 steps to remember as you go through this process.

1 – Name it, but don't explain it. Like I mentioned earlier, different feelings will have different sensations. Pinpoint what bubbles up when you ask "How am I feeling?" but don't give it a story. The fact is, the longer you've been suppressing feelings the more you have imprisoned inside you, and this particular one might have been generated decades ago. There's no point trying to find the story associated with that emotion because this bout of anxiety stayed long after the story was forgotten. Just say, "Hello, anxiety." "Hello fear." "Hello sadness." Focus on figuring out which feeling it is and welcome its presence.

2 – Relax. Anxiety, sadness, anger, fear. These tend to be feelings that rile you up, but in this case you're going to deal with them differently because you're the one in control. So while you're letting the feelings roll up on you and take over your physical body, relax. Again, don't try to find the story. Instead, just let yourself fully melt into the physical sensations while maintaining your calm state of mind. The whole point of this exercise is unloading your emotions while staying calm. Welcome the effects they have on your torso, let them have their moment truly and fully, and keep your mind focused on the present moment inside that sweet spot. Relax your shoulders, your neck, unclench your hands and stomach. Keep cycling through your body and releasing any tension you find.

3 – Breathe. Remember, slowwwww, deeeeep breaths. Those negative feelings will fill your body up, make it feel heavy and bloated and squeezed, but I want you to keep breathing past and through those sensations. Keep drawing your breath deep down to the bottom of your belly. It might feel like your emotions are taking up so much room it's hard to breathe, but that's an illusion. Fill your lungs, relax, slowly exhale, relax.

4 – Surrender. Fully immerse yourself into whatever emotion is running through you. This isn't the time to try to control those emotions. This is the time to fetch them up thoroughly. Do not try to minimize, reduce, or cut short what's popping up. You need to do the opposite. Otherwise, you're missing the point of finally getting them out. Yes, they'll feel uncomfortable. Yes, you'll be tempted to try to explain or pin them on something you can remember. Don't. Just surrender to them, allow them, and express them while sitting calmly in your chair.

You're going to think this is the strangest thing at first, you sitting there looking so serene on the outside while your insides are upheaving. But let me tell you after doing this a few times you're going to think this is the best thing since sliced bread. Identify what comes up, say hello to it, relax into it, breathe through it, surrender fully to the sensations, and finally...

5 – Seek out the last little bit. When you feel like the feeling you've brought up has gone through the majority of its expulsion, go get that last shred. Say you brought up a feeling of anxiety. You felt it converge in the pit of your stomach and collect in there like stones. Hot and heavy, that anxiety seemed to take over your insides, getting bigger and bigger till it felt like all you were comprised of was a big hot mess of anxiety. You stayed relaxed and breathed through that mess, and as it developed it seemed to eventually begin to rise through your body, squeezing your lungs and choking your throat as it passed upwards. Eventually you felt the physical effects lessen as it slowly dissipated out the top of your head, like gas escaping out of you and releasing its pressure. But for good measure, let's conduct a root canal on that sucker and make sure every last bit is brought forth and removed. This isn't to say the next emotion you bring up won't be anxiety again, but whatever case this specific bout of anxiety is related to is going to be fully expressed, right here, right now.

So once again, go into the pit of your stomach, relax, and seek. Find the last shred and let it run its course through your body, letting it build and then escape through the top of your head. Trust me, you'll know when it's done.

Repeat this process a few more times if you have time. But if you've got 20 minutes to meditate before your next appointment just fetching one will work wonders too. Be sure to cycle through a feeling completely, so that you can come back to a space of serenity before you end your session for the day. Let your mind and body rest comfortably in that space for a few minutes, so what you're bringing forth with you when you get up is the calm comfort that comes with creating positive changes in your brain. It's such an amazing win/win.

CHAPTER 9

No More Hoover Dam

What the hell has happened in our society that women feel they have to swallow their tears all the time? Without fail, every client who comes to me because she just can't seem to sort out her love life needs a lesson on how to conduct a good cry.

Seriously!

And you know what? I actually learned how when I was almost 40. Crazy. We should have been taught by our mothers, aunts, and grandmothers that it's okay to let all our emotions out but instead the cycle of holding back our true feelings can go back generations.

And we wonder why we're emotionally wounded and have trouble connecting with those we love.

It's time for us to stop this cycle. This is the moment to become true women, able to feel and express everything inside of us instead of bottling up our feelings for the sake of appearing unflappable. Because you know what? All those negative emotions that you've trapped inside are having the opposite effect. They are eating away at your guts like rust, slowly disintegrating you from the inside out. And one day you're going to collapse, because what was supposed to be strong has been eroded until it couldn't support itself any longer.

But it's not too late.

There's a repair crew waiting on the sidelines, and they're highly talented and capable. With your help this whole erosion can be turned around and you can be rebuilt stronger than ever.

Exciting, right?

So let me teach you the power of your tears, because if you don't know the importance of crying then you're rusting out from all the moisture trapped inside.

Your tears are your emotional detox, and if you're letting them flow, and I mean *flow*, then you're cleansing your emotions and allowing yourself to stay strong.

Sounds counter intuitive doesn't it? Cry, and you'll be strong. Don't cry, and you'll be weak. But consider this: Compare how much you cry (and I'm not talking about a tear leaked here and there, I mean big sobbing convulsing cries) to how healthy you feel emotionally. Chances are, the less you're crying the unhappier you are.

Just like all those negative emotions you push down day in and day out are still trapped inside you even decades later, so are all the tears you've pushed back. They're piling up, and now you wonder why there's no room for happiness. It's because you've been all filled up, my dear. It's time to blow up that Hoover Dam and let the water behind it rush out, because each drop that leaves is a little more room in you for something better.

Which is what you want, right? Room inside you to fill with newer, better emotions. Like love, happiness, joy, appreciation, gratitude... contentment. Mmmmmm. I just got a warm fuzzy saying those words.

So, here's the funny part. I'm going to actually teach you how to cry. Yeah, you might think you already know how. But maybe you need a little insight and permission into what crying is really supposed to be, because no one ever sat you down and said, "Listen, doing it like this is really okay."

Feeling water well up and fill your eyes, getting a knot in your throat, and having a few tears fall isn't crying. It's just the beginning, and if you don't follow through you're not releasing anything. It's kind of like feeling a turtlehead in your bum (gross, I know, I just couldn't think of a better analogy). You have a poop there, and it's letting you know it's there, but if you don't sit down and let it happen it's still there. And if you never let it happen, you're just getting more and more backed up and all that poop is going to make you sick.

Do you get it? Crying and letting it all out is normal, and it's also necessary. You've got to do it.

So how do you cry in a way that's normal, necessary, and cleansing?

By surrendering to it.

Think about the last time you threw up. Sure, you probably fought the very idea for as long as you could, but once it became imminent what did you do? You prepared, didn't you? You accepted the fact that it was going to happen, and you got ready to surrender to the act itself.

You tied your hair back if it was long. You went to the bathroom and lifted the lid and seat. If you're like me, you did a quick cleanup of the toilet bowl cause, yuck. And then you hunkered down and let it happen.

You relaxed, and you didn't fight the rolling and heaving of your insides. And when the majority of it seemed to have passed, you gave it a moment longer to see if there was just a bit more heaving left to do.

Crying should be exactly the same. I mean, there was a reason why you threw up, wasn't there? You ate something bad, or you caught a bug. Something caused a rejection of what was inside your body, and your smart digestive system said, "This has got to go, because if I let it stay it's just going to cause damage."

Change your view on crying and start seeing it as your system alerting you that something inside you is toxic and needs to be expelled. You need to give your system credit for being smarter than your conditioning, and respond to it. Let those tears flow, and not just a little. A lot. Till the last bit is out of you.

So what does that look like? Well, a lot like throwing up.

You'll feel physical sensations happening inside your body, and instead of fighting them you need to relax and let them happen. I understand that this isn't something you really want to do in front of people, so find opportunities. I had a client with two jobs and three kids who would unleash her tears when she'd be alone in her car.

Relax, relax, relax. It's important to remember this. Surrender to what your body wants to do, and go with the flow. You're going to heave, your face is going to scrunch up, your head is going to drop, your body is going to fold. Go with it, and fight nothing.

Let your breath come in great, big, deep, body shaking sobs. Let yourself wail if that's coming. Relax, and let yourself go deep into your belly, see your invisible hands scooping inside of you, fetching everything that's there.

Let it take you to the ground. I'll often end up on all fours, hunched over like a dog yacking up what it shouldn't have eaten. Let this process take over your body, and if you end up sobbing in a fetal position on the floor, good! It means you're allowing yourself to be real.

Don't be afraid of what happens to you when you blow up that dam. You've got a lot trapped inside of you and frankly, it's going to be pretty intense for a while. Think about it. If I strapped some dynamite on the Hoover Dam and blew that sucker up there'd be a ton of rushing water at the beginning, but as more and more water is released the pressure subsides, and eventually everything trapped behind it has flowed out. Now all that's coming is just the normal flow of water that happens throughout the seasons.

When I first started letting it all out I was crying several times a day. And I'm not talking sitting quietly while tears fell. I mean big, convulsing, down on my hands and knees crying. I was releasing twenty years of loss from the death of my sister. I was releasing thirty plus years of sadness regarding my relationship with my parents. I was releasing two years of grief from the death of my cat, who I considered my life changer. And so much more. I was letting it all out, one cry at a time.

And it took time. Once I started crying it was just the beginning, because I had so much trapped inside of me. I cried every day for so long that when days started happening when breaking down and sobbing on my knees didn't take place, it was a novelty. "I didn't cry today, baby," I'd say to my husband when he came home at night and asked how my day went. Not because I was proud that I held my tears back, but just because not crying was something different to report.

You don't have to tell anyone you're crying a lot now. This can be between you and you, but you've got to let those tears out. For your sake and for the sake of those you love. Because holding them back isn't serving you at all, and ultimately your suffering spills over into expressions of anger and frustration and it ends up contaminating your relationships.

Crying doesn't just liberate you. It liberates everyone around you too.

CHAPTER 10

Only You Can Prevent Forest Fires

It's time for you to take responsibility for your emotions. This isn't a blame thing, this is a reality check. Your blasting amygdala and long repressed emotions are like a fiery volcano inside of you, and that combination is blasting red hot lava far and wide, splashing and burning you and everyone around you.

We have this habit of looking around and trying to pin a source for every time our feelings catch fire, but the fact is sometimes it's all in our heads. Listen, I'm not saying people aren't pissing you off. I guarantee they are, people are like that and sometimes we're unintentional assholes. But sometimes it really isn't them. Sometimes, it's you. And I want you to become aware of the distinction so you can not only have appropriate outbursts, but constructive ones too.

Remember the story of the boy who cried wolf? People just started tuning him out, and the one time he was really, truly in distress they'd become immune to his words and nobody came to help. I don't want this for you. I want people to really hear you and come to your aid because you deserve it. But in order for that to happen you need to know the difference between what's real and what's just your brain shooting off.

When your amygdala is over-active it sends signals to your nervous system that feels like a reaction. Fight or flight, right? So cortisol and adrenaline are released into your body, making you feel stressed and/or anxious, and your first compulsion is to ask yourself, "Who pissed me off? Who do I need to address and what do I need to say to them so they stop making me feel this way?"

I want you to hear this with an open mind: You're not always right.

Sometimes, those feelings are just your brain, and looking for a cause to address is just perpetuating that reaction, strengthening it, like going to the gym and exercising your muscles, prepping you for a bigger reaction the next time.

Yes, meditating will help you reduce the severity, and the more you meditate the less intensely you'll feel those reactions. But you also need to use your logical mind to deal with these flare ups because you're human, and being human means being emotional and hormonal and sometimes, just off center.

A great relationship is filled with allowances, and it has to begin with you. Allow yourself to be off sometimes without looking for a story to ascribe to the feeling. Allow yourself to have bad days, to have mood swings, to feel grumpy or hormonal or bitchy.

Here's the thing. You can have the feeling without having an outward reaction. You can have the emotion without looking for something outside of yourself to pin it on. You can experience angst without doing anything more than saying to yourself, "Huh, I'm feeling _____ right now." You can acknowledge your feelings, and best of all, you can own them and move on. Because a lot of them, more than you know, are just blips in your brain.

Which is liberating to realize. Think of how much less emotional pain you'll feel when you just let the moment pass without turning to someone and igniting a heated debate over who started it.

Let me paint you two scenarios.

Scenario 1 – You have a moment where stress and anxiety rise up on your drive to work. You quickly run through your memory banks and come up with how your man didn't pick up toilet paper on the way home last night. You fume over how irresponsible he is, how thoughtless he's consistently been, how you just can't rely on him to do anything right. Like a naughty parrot, your mind begins repeating that message over and over all day long. "What a jerk! What a jerk!"

By the time you get home (picking up some toilet paper on the way) you're in anger overdrive. The first thing you do when you see him is toss the toilet paper in his direction. "Here!" you say, "I did this today cause I sure as hell can't count on you to do one simple thing!"

He lashes out in retaliation. Or stomps off to his man cave. Either way, you're fighting, and the battle lasts well into tomorrow. Maybe into next week. Maybe it never ends, because before you make up from this one something else gets you angry.

Scenario 2 – You have a moment where stress and anxiety rise up on your drive to work. You don't give it a story. Instead you take a moment to let the feeling cycle through your body. Using the exercise you've been practicing during meditation, you relax your body, deepen your breathing, and let your brain go blank a bit. You let the sensations fill you up, then rise and dissipate. After a few minutes you feel calm again, and you turn up the volume and bop away to the Bruno Mars song on the radio.

You pick up toilet paper on the way home and give your man a hug and kiss when you see him. He thinks, "Wow, what an awesome woman I have. She so could have given me crap about forgetting the toilet paper, but she didn't." His mind begins to seek something he can do to make you happy because his mood is gratitude, and he remembers how you mentioned last week that the kitchen faucet was loose.

He gets his toolbox and fixes it after supper. You see him doing this, asscrack and all, and love him to bits for looking for ways to take care of you. You tell him warmly, "Thanks, baby, you're such a good man!" He kisses you tenderly, cocks his head back to look you in the eye, and says "Well, I've got a pretty awesome woman myself."

Which story left you feeling warm and fuzzy? Which life do you want to live?

I'm not saying there won't be real issues that give rise to feelings of anger and frustration, stuff that stresses you out and needs to be dealt with and addressed. And I'm going to give you the tools to handle those in a way that brings you both closer together. But all too often we mistake our blitzing brain for something that's an issue, and all we end up doing is trying to deal with one issue after another. And do you know what you end up with? A relationship that feels like it's filled with nothing but issues.

Do you know what it's like to be in a relationship and not fight? Ever? I do, and it's pretty freaking awesome. I used to agree when people said, "Everybody fights sometimes" and "It's normal for couples to fight," but now I don't because I had learned that even if you've been through years and years of constant hurt, anger, and battles like we did, you can still master the tools that turn the whole thing around and maintain daily love and peace in your relationship.

Let me tell you, our relationship deteriorated to the point where my man started sleeping at his shop, and if I can learn how to come back from that so can you. And here's the kicker, the process by which you accomplish all this feels so emotionally healing for you. You feel calmer, happier, and you and your partner become closer than you can imagine right now. Think honeymoon period, but every day. This is the part that I call "magical."

Because love and appreciation and kindness and caring, and the accompanying kisses and cuddles and sweet words, all become part of your everyday lives together. And isn't that what you're looking for? Yearning for? Striving for?

So let's do it.

CHAPTER 11

Who's the Wizard? You're the Wizard!

P

You, and only you, are in charge of the direction your relationships go. If you're starting a sentence with "Well, he ___" you're literally giving up your power.

He might well be a douche, but how you feel about his douchey behaviour or how you react to it is within your power to control. Shrinking your amygdala through meditation means his bad behaviours won't set you off. Increasing your hippocampus through meditation means you'll have more insight as to why either of you are acting out, and you'll let more of your collective "off" moments slide by.

Releasing your pent up emotions during meditation means they don't infect your relationship, and allowing those that pop up run their course means they won't get trapped inside of you, adding up until you explode.

There's a lot more I'm going to teach you, but this is the foundation. This is what makes the rest fall neatly into place and get so much easier.

This is not an overnight thing but it's your commitment and consistency to a change in your own behaviours and making meditation and crying a part of your routine that'll carry you from where you are now to where you want to be. You got this, girl! You deserve the happiness doing what's in this book will bring you. You deserve a life filled with joy and love. You deserve a man who loves you to bits and shows you how much he cares. You deserve everything you want; you just have to do a few simple things to achieve your desires.

And please, don't tell me you don't have time. Because that reasoning is exactly what's going to keep you on this same path of emotional erosion. Give yourself the gift of doing what's in this book. It's what you need.

Step 2 – Clarity

Immerse yourself in your existence.

CHAPTER 12

Perspective is Everything

I used to say men were less emotional than women (Hey, don't judge me, scientists used to say the world was flat. People make mistakes). I even had a theory that it helped them be good cavemen, seeing as it was more their job to go out and kill, and having a lower capacity for emotion helped them drive a spear through Bambi without the depth of remorse we women would suffer.

Well, it turned out I was wrong, and I found out just in the nick of time. See, my blindness to just how deeply men feel was an Achilles heel in our relationship because I had no idea how much my actions affected my man, and it wasn't until we were on the virtual edge of a complete meltdown that I came across a study that dove into men's responses to four categories of emotions – blissful, funny, excited, and heartwarming.

It turned out he was just better at hiding his emotions than I was, and my newfound insight saved the day and gave me the right response when I asked him to come home. "What's changed?" he asked, and I said the words he was waiting to hear. "I have much more respect for your feelings."

"I'm happy to hear that, baby," he said. I could tell from his tone that a huge weight had instantly lifted for him, and I was glad my insight could make him happy. I'd been wrong, but it's better to eventually get it right than stay wrong forever.

The way you view what happens in your relationship is everything. And I mean everything. Unfortunately, we wear goggles most of the time, and we can't help it. We have ego goggles, hurt goggles, pain goggles, past history goggles, what our friends told us goggles, doubt goggles, and of course the good ol' "How I wish it was" goggles.

All these different goggles have their way of changing the world we see and deeply impact how we navigate relationships. Some are cloudy, some are prescription but the wrong prescription, some are cracked, and some are just plain dirty. When it comes to love and maintaining a healthy relationship all the goggles need to come off. Otherwise, we're trapped behind a lens skewing our vision, and ultimately we're just stumbling around blindly, trying to make good decisions.

But you can't remove those goggles without embracing the three most important words you can exchange in a relationship. No, I'm not talking about "I love you." I'm talking about the most healing words either you or your man will ever say to each other.

"I was wrong."

Wooooo! Boy, I could feel you clench all the way over here! Lol!

I know you've probably spent some time spinning tight circles around your reasoning, and I don't blame you. It's what our brains are constructed to do, because being aware of how often we're off base can be damaging to our self-esteem, and we're finely tuned machines built to run efficiently. It's important that our brains maintain a certain illusion so we can boldly go forth into this world without being weighed down by a constant bombardment of negative self-judgement.

Basically, what I'm saying is we're wrong much more often than we think. Usually this doesn't interfere with our day to day lives because the majority of the things we're wrong about are minor and do little to interfere with our needs, goals, and desires. But when it comes to the daily dealings with our partners sometimes the things we're wrong about drive a big wedge between us and can cause some pretty big issues. Not being aware of just how deep my man's feelings ran contributed to a lot more wrongs, all of which I was glossing over as I looked through my "I know what's right" goggles.

But the reality was my wrongness was driving him farther and farther away.

Being wrong is normal, and finding out you're wrong doesn't have to pose a challenge. See, that clench you felt when I proposed that maybe you weren't as right as you thought you were was just your ego, and while your brain is made to build and maintain your self-esteem so you have the strength and guts to tackle this world, your ego colludes with your brain to confirm the notion that yeah, you got balls, and big ones at that.

It's your ego that lights a flame under your emotions at the very notion that you're not sitting on the right side of a fight. It's like your brain is a castle, and your ego is the guardsman. The thing is your ego doesn't distinguish what's happening in the real world, and it's the dumbest bouncer you'll ever meet. Regardless of who shows up at the gate, from dignitaries to beggars, it's going to shove everyone back and tell them to eff off.

But you see, you need some of these people to get through the gates. Visiting royalty can enhance your empire, making you richer with their gifts of gold and expanding your dynasty by offering one of their princes up for marriage. If you let that big, dumb ol' bouncer run the door to your castle he's going to turn the wrong people away and you're going to end up sitting in your tower all by yourself, growing your Rapunzel hair in the hopes that one day someone will be able to circumvent that dumbass and finally make you happy.

Fire that bouncer and replace him with someone smarter... you.

How? Easy. Remember how you learned that sometimes the anxiety and fear that rises inside you is just your brain shooting off reactions for, sometimes, no good reason, and you can just let the moment pass without letting it cause drama for you? It's the same idea with that flash of rightness.

And frankly, it's healthy to analyze what's going on when your ego sets off a fire inside you because that inner heat lets you know something in your reality is colliding with your opinions.

Acknowledging you're not always right is the first step to creating and maintaining a healthy relationship, and using your emotions to gauge what you should be looking deeper into is using your critical thinking cap to ensure you're not getting in your own way.

It's funny, because once I started analyzing my reality every time my ego flared up and stopped needing to be right all the time we stopped fighting. And it was about six months into that process that I heard him say to someone, "She's fully renovated." And you know what? I was proud of that moment. What he was saying was I'd stopped bulldozing over his feelings and started owning my faults, and he couldn't be more content.

And frankly, I was happy too! I mean, think about it. There was no more discord in our relationship, no more fights simmering under the surface, no more words spinning in my brain looking for their escape path. My mind was free to delve into happiness, and into peace.

You know, I did a lot of research in my quest for spiritual answers, and in my opinion the Bible says it best: "The truth will set you free." And it absolutely does. Finally, free to be happy.

CHAPTER 13

Change Takes Time

So a little while back I changed where I stored my toothbrush. It used to be in the linen cupboard beside the bathroom vanity, and for almost a full year I'd open the door a few times a day and pull it out. And then one day I got tired of trying to delicately extract my facecloths from behind the glass it was in and I put the toothbrush holder on the counter, right beside the faucet.

And then, for months after I kept opening that cupboard even though my toothbrush was right beside the tap I'd just turned.

When we do something often enough we create a channel in our neural pathways and our thought process starts running on auto pilot, taking us down the same path over and over even when we've made a conscious decision to take a left turn instead of a right from now on.

Which is why forgiveness is a huge asset in any relationship because honestly, being human means making mistakes, even despite ourselves. It just comes with the territory.

You need to get really good at forgiveness in order to find

happiness because the opposite of forgiveness is blame and punishment. And the best place to start practicing is right here, with yourself.

You have to forgive yourself for all your mistakes, whether they're as big as misjudging your man's feelings or as small as opening the wrong cupboard when you reach for the toothbrush. You have to learn to be soft with yourself, because once you master that and become proficient at quickly moving on and moving forward you're going to extend that towards the people you love.

Think of forgiveness as a super power.

Now I'm pretty good at using this super power because I've been practicing. You, well, you're going to do a little crashing around for a while till you figure out how to steer yourself in mid-air. But that's okay, everything new has a learning curve, right? Just know that the more you practice the more it become second nature, and if you want this power to work for you bad enough you'll stick with it till it gets easy. And it does.

So be gentle with yourself. Often. It's important that you accept your flaws and lack of knowledge, and equally important that you not beat yourself up over them. Give yourself space to learn, and forgive yourself for anything you've been wrong about and anything you *will* be wrong about. The faster your make forgiveness trump ego and guilt the faster you'll move through issues, turning what would have normally been big deals into tiny blips.

Listen, you deserve forgiveness. Loads and loads of it. And you'd want your man to forgive you easily when you get it wrong. But it's not fair to ask for anything you're not willing to give first, and that applies here too. If you don't learn to forgive yourself you'll block the notion that you can be forgiven by those that love you, and you'll end up spinning round and round in a negative cycle of "I'm shitty." You're not shitty. You're human, and it's okay to make mistakes. The key is learning from them and reminding yourself to do better next time.

CHAPTER 14

The Purpose of Negative Feelings

People suck sometimes. I suck, you suck, and he sucks too. We all suck at one point or another, and honestly, sucking is just part of growth. We need to get it wrong so we can fully realize what right is. I mean, would you really be able to define what's hot if you never experience what's cold?

Consider this. I once studied the Sudanese who escaped civil war from their country of Sudan and eventually settled in Maine, USA. Their homeland was a steaming hot place, and they'd never experienced anything as chilly as a Maine winter. For them "cold" was something around 60 degrees Fahrenheit. So can you imagine when they felt their first winter at 25 degrees? You can bet they had a new interpretation of cold after that.

What I'm saying is, when you open yourself up to new experiences you can learn whole new depths and definitions to what you thought you'd already figured out.

With that being said, the suckage we suffer when we invite people into our lives are really just emotional triggers, and those triggers can serve a purpose. They can highlight the baggage we're carrying around that's straining our sore neck and shoulder muscles. They can magnify the insecurities and fears that are blowing up our amygdala. They can shine a light into the dark corners of our souls where demons are gleefully wringing their hands at the havoc they wreak on our well-being, and spiders are spinning thick webs designed to trap any happiness trying to seep through.

Your triggers are your friends, not your foes. Your emotions are your beacons, they are the voices in your head letting you know "This needs your attention." They are your guides, your Sherpas, your spirits of previous experiences waiting to be acknowledged and told they're free to go to the light.

Embrace your feelings. You always have a choice when your feelings pop up. Will you unthinkingly react to them? Or will you pause and take a moment to reflect on what sort of lesson they're trying to teach you?

Here's the thing about choosing the right man to have a relationship with. The space you create between the two of you, as unsettled as it feels sometimes, is actually the safe space in which you can do the most growing.

Now here's the thing – growth normally comes wrapped up inside a bunch of angst. Look at all the motivational speakers out there, from Oprah to Maya Angelou and even Tony Robbins. They'll all say their biggest growth came from pretty tumultuous times, and it was a choice to either sink down into despair or rise above and become a better human being.

So here you are with someone who's committed to standing by you through thick and thin. You've circled the wagons, so to speak, and it's you two against the world. Sure, inside that circle it feels like you're pitted against each other, but maybe that upheaval is what's necessary to crack through your walls and break through to who you really want to be.

Listen, growth hurts. Like, a lot. It breaks you down, tears you apart, and shreds you to your very core so you can recreate yourself bigger and stronger than before. Ever go to the gym and work out so hard you had trouble moving the next day? That was your muscle fiber that literally tore itself, and the soreness you felt over the next few days was the healing process. More muscle fiber was created to fill in the tears, and when you hit the gym the following week you had the capability to lift heavier weights.

Same thing when it comes to your spirit. Embrace lifting what feels heavy, work through the pain, and you'll be set to deal with even heavier stuff going forward.

See this relationship is your emotional gym. Relationships should be the place where people come to sweat it out, grunt, groan, and push themselves so they can change in some form. This is your opportunity to unpack, grow, and step beyond your fears while standing in a loving, supportive space. No, it doesn't always feel loving and supportive when you're battling through some pretty big disagreements, but at the end of the day both of you hope that you'll make it through this and find a better space together. That's what I call love and support. A willingness to stay, even when it gets hard.

The key here is being sure to choose the right man to go through all this with. I wrote a book called *No More Assholes* that helps define if he's a man with guts and long term vision or a guy who's looking for scapegoats to pin his problems and responsibilities on while seeking someone to service him, without regard to his partner's emotional needs. If you're wondering who you're with, give that a read. But for the sake of this book, I'm going to assume you've picked yourself a good man and just need help working through the sticky stuff.

CHAPTER 15

Unclench

Now here's the thing – you'll never get to the other side of your emotions, from a negative place to a positive place, until you quit holding them back. And while half the battle is releasing them when you're alone and letting your tears and associated feelings flow, you also need to allow your feelings to show in front of him too.

Why? Because his lizard brain needs that level of communication in order to be able to respond appropriately.

See, you're not doing yourself any favours by *not* crying in front of him. He needs to know how much you trust him with your feelings because if he's not getting that sign a part of him isn't fully tuned into you, and that lack of fine tuning is interfering with your level of intimacy with each other.

And it's only within intimacy that you'll be able to unpack all that baggage and be done with it once and for all.

I spent yeeeaaaarrrrsssss not showing my man my tears. And do you know what happened? We spent an equal amount of time not getting anywhere. It was like two solid steel walls trying to push past each other and get to the other side. Flat up against each other, pushing and pushing but neither being able to gain an inch because each was a solid, immovable force railing against a solid and immovable force.

It didn't matter what I said or how much I explained my feelings. It didn't matter how much I fought to be understood, I just couldn't seem to get through and get him to understand what I needed.

And then one day out of sheer frustration and surrender I broke down, and it was like he was suddenly seeing me in a whole new light. He started showing me more understanding and compassion, and he started working with me to help solve problems.

And this begs the question: Why do men need to see us cry in order to be better plugged in to finding solutions?

Here's my theory.

Take my hand, and let's step into the time machine again and visit our ancestors two hundred thousand years ago. I like to study them and ask myself why something that seems to work today would be a part of our evolutionary process.

Now crying isn't something new to us as a species, and it's not even exclusive to us. Elephants have been known to cry when they mourn a lost member of their herd, rhesus monkeys cry when separated from their mothers. Crying when emotional is a normal part of our biology, while not crying seems to be a part of our culture.

But over and over I've seen how crying brings men closer

to their women emotionally. Why? I think it comes down to trust.

See, when our ancestors walked this earth they did so in a time that was a helluva lot more dangerous than today. We weren't at the top of the food chain, and we had to keep a sharp eye out for predators. Otherwise, we'd be lunch. We also had to keep a keen ear cocked to noises that didn't fit the daily drone of what wouldn't hurt us, like a twig snapping under a heavy paw. In essence, we had to spend a lot of time on the lookout.

Now think about what happens when you let loose and cry. Your tears keep you from seeing straight, and your sobbing overrides any soft sounds. You would be super vulnerable to attack if you didn't choose to cry in a safe environment, and his brain knows that. So when you allow yourself to cry in his presence his instinct to protect you kicks in, and knowing you trust him to ensure nothing hurts you in this vulnerable time sends a signal that deep down you've chosen him as the man you entrust with your very survival.

That, to him, is an honor. Just the very notion builds him up emotionally and gives him a sense of purpose within this relationship. He feels important and vital, as any protector would. And dear reader, isn't trust everything in a relationship? How close would you feel to your man if you thought that deep down he didn't trust you?

Your tears are the ultimate sign, bigger than any words you

could ever say, that you trust your man completely. And when he knows you trust him that much it can only go up from there.

Now here's another relationship building block that's stacked in your favour when you let your tears show. It teaches him that emotions are acceptable in your relationship, and he starts to unclench his own.

Your poor man has probably been conditioned to swallow his feelings and hide them behind a wall. And chances are it's a message that's even more deeply ingrained than yours because he's been hearing "big boys don't cry" throughout his lifetime.

Men aren't just told to suck it up and stuff it down; it's also part of their DNA to stuff it down in order to "get the job done." From the start of our evolution they've had to put their feelings aside in order to ensure the survival of their offspring. Cavemen who didn't twist a fluffy bunny's neck to feed his mate and baby didn't get to reproduce, and not going out to hunt effectively because he was having an "off day" just didn't jive. My own husband regularly disregards his stress and fatigue because running a business to support his family comes first, even before himself. It's the way of the caveman.

But stuffing their emotions doesn't mean they don't exist, and letting him know you feel safe enough within your union to let yours show is your way of leading by example. Once he sees you're willing to take down the façade and be real he'll be more apt to allow himself to break down too, and in this way both of you can ultimately be rebuilt better and stronger. And when you take your newfound strengths and combine them, well, wow.

But this whole thing is a process. It doesn't happen overnight, and you'll both be going forward in fits and starts. You'll take two steps forward, he'll take one. He'll take two forward, and you'll take one backwards. It's all a dance, and sometimes you'll lead, sometimes he will, sometimes you'll be in sync and sometimes you'll step on each other's toes.

But don't give up because if you maintain a dedication to growth and overcoming all your obstacles eventually you'll master the Tango, often referred to as one of the most difficult dances out there.

CHAPTER 16

What Are You Really Fighting About?

When it comes to fights, when you get to the meat of the matter you can usually boil it down to a few different topics. Here they are.

1 – Read my mind. "Read my miiiiiiind," my ex-husband used to say when we'd figure out that the fight we were having was just plain dumb. You know the one, where one of you gets pissy because you communicated half of what you wanted, then got mad when ESP didn't transmit the rest. It's a common thing we do with each other, and I often hear women and men say, "They should just know."

"I want him to light candles and give me a massage to get things rolling from time to time!" she'll say to her friends (and not to him), then get angry when he simply turns to her while they're watching TV and says, "Well baby, I'm showered, and I've digested my supper. Want to get it on?"

There are a lot of things you can, and should, ask from your man, but reading your mind isn't one of them. Next time you find yourself feeling frustrated with him ask yourself this crucial question: Have I clearly and lovingly communicated exactly what I'm looking for from him and most importantly, have I led the way?

I worked with a couple recently where she complained about that scenario. So I asked her, "When was the last time you lit candles and gave him a massage?" She couldn't remember. See, men are apt students, but you've got to show them, not tell them, and certainly not *not* tell them and then expect them to get it right. That's not fair.

So guess what she did? She lit some candles and gave him a sexy massage, and do you know what he's been doing ever since? Lighting candles, giving her pre-sex massages, and taking her out to buy sexy toys to boot.

Teach your man what you want by leading by example and using your words. It's the clearest form of communication you can have.

2 – *Expectations*. Expectations are a huge relationship killer. We create this story in our heads about how things ought to be, and then start to feel disappointment when the storyboards in our imaginations don't play out in real life. But relationships aren't stories. They're being enacted in real time, and the sooner you ground yourself in reality and see what you have instead of what you wish for, the happier you'll be.

Why? Because you'll start seeing what he's doing instead of what you're not getting.

I'll give you an example. I had a long standing client let me know she thought her man was going to propose to her on their yearly cottage getaway. "I'm sure he's going to pop the question. He's being sneaky lately, and he's saying we're going to rough it instead of getting our usual cottage." So she went on this trip, all prepared to say "Yes!" Two days in she messaged me: "No proposal yet."

I told her to release her expectations.

But by the end of the trip she'd worked herself up into a high state of disappointment, and instead of thanking him for getting a beautiful deluxe cottage (the surprise he'd been sneaky about) she complained about the amount of money they'd spent. Both of them suffered lingering misery over the trip because she hadn't gotten what he hadn't planned, and he never got the thank you he'd been seeking when he'd put together the extravagant affair.

So instead of enjoying a beautiful upgrade on their tradition and letting him bask in the afterglow of making her happy, both of them ended up feeling a funk because her expectations put a damper on the whole thing. Now when you think about this, how much is he going to be thinking about proposing after she gave him grief for spending money on their trip while silently fuming he hadn't spent money on a ring? What would you think is going through his mind? That he should plan something again to make her happy or not plan anything anymore because nothing seems to make her happy?

Expectations drive a wedge between you and what you want.

You need to be fluid when it comes to your relationship and let things progress and flow. I often say, change your behaviour to match your goals, but release the outcome. Don't let expectations create negative emotions.

3 – You're not listening. "I feel like I'm not being heard. It doesn't matter how many times I've told him, (fill in the blank) doesn't change. He never listens to me when I try to talk about something." Have you been saying this? Do you find that every time you try to resolve something it turns into an ugly fight where you're both doing the "yeah but you" routine?

It's pretty typical, and trust me, I've been there, done that. It's soooooo frustrating when you've bided your time and tried to wait for the best moment to bring up something that's crawling around inside your mind, only to be shut down with his impervious wall of "yeah but you."

Then you try to steer the conversation back to your point, and he keeps up his end of trying to get his own agenda heard. And guess what he's thinking when you both just completely shut down or dissolve into another meltdown?

"I feel like I'm not being heard. It doesn't matter how many times I've told her, (fill in the blank) doesn't change. She never listens to me when I try to talk about something."

Round and round it goes, till you both get dizzy and fall down. And maybe puke.

But there's a way around this, and it's a throwback to one of the first lessons we learned as kids: Wait your turn. I know, I know! You want to go first, and you feel you have every right to go first. I'm not gonna argue that. But what if being heard means going second, and that's the only option on the table? Your ego might reject the notion, but your ego isn't your friend.

If fact, your ego isn't looking out for you at all. It wants to be right and that's all, and it doesn't care one bit whether or not that's going to work out for you. So when your ego asks, "Why should he go first?!" you want to put that sucker away in the single sock drawer and ask yourself what's really important here – being heard or being first?

Because I assure you, until you take the wind out of his sails there isn't a thing he's going to hear over the whooshing air around his head.

Which leads me to…

4 – *You don't get me.* What hurts more than feeling like the person you're in a relationship with has no idea who you are? Not much.

Feeling misunderstood is a miserable feeling when you're living with someone. It tears at your self-esteem because you're fighting against being dragged down by any negative views your partner has of you. It turns your emotions into dead weights, making it hard to feel anything positive towards him and your union in general.

It occurred to me a long time ago that we seek to be understood. It's a yearning we have deep inside to be *seen*, and lacking that we tend to feel like we're floating isolated and friendless in a life raft, far out in the ocean. It's a very lonely feeling.

All this reminds me of my little Lulu. I'm the most important, beloved person in the world for her because I understand she's under socialized and often feels insecure. I know she needs special consideration when I take her to public places, and I'm gentle when I handle her. I don't bulldoze over her personality. I take it into consideration and do my best to make her life better by taking her everywhere and having treats for people to give her so she can learn to trust more and more.

I understand her needs and I respect them, and that's huge in any relationship. Exercising your curiosity and investing time to get to know who your partner is deep down inside and using that knowledge to make their life better in a multitude of little ways pays huge dividends in a relationship.

Again, I can hear your ego all the way over here. "What about me? Shouldn't he be looking for ways to make me happy?" Yes! Yes he should. So show him how that learning process takes place.

Look for little things like making coffee in the morning, tossing mini versions of his favourite chocolate bar in his lunch bag, asking if there's anything he needs when you go out, or putting his clean clothes away in his drawers. Consider these little things to be your emotional gifts, and like gifts give them freely without making a fuss.

Women undervalue the effect these small things have on their man's psyche. They don't realize that a grateful man puts his thinking cap on and starts to seek out ways to make his woman as happy as he is, if not happier. And when he does, always say thank you, because a man who feels his woman appreciates his efforts does even more.

And the most important ingredient in this dish? Telling him what a good man he is and how happy his efforts make you. See, men are programmed to look for happiness in our faces because back in caveman days a happy woman raised a thriving baby, and although we're thousands of generations past our early ancestors we still have a lot of the same procreation and survival instincts. He's still driven to want to make you happy, and letting him know he scored raises his emotional level, and now you're both on an upswing.

It's an awesome place to be, when you're both investing in each other's happiness and feeling like your partner sees you, gets you, and wants to do the things that give you pleasure.

But here's what'll get in your way...

5 – *Nobody wants to be the hero.* For anything to start, someone has to be the first to step into the ring. Now I agree it would be awesome if he was the one initiating all this, but how likely is it that your man is going to pick up a self-help book and start reading it?

Relationships fail when both people get into "me first" mode and refuse to budge. And that clenching you feel when you consider being the first to break out of that stance and put some effort into making him happy before he makes you happy? That's your ego again. And you might think your ego likes you, but it doesn't. Your ego isn't friends with anybody but itself, so beware of putting much stock into what it says you should do.

If anything is going to change in your relationship someone needs to change first. Otherwise, you're both continuing to spin round and round the same issues, nonstop. If you don't break the pattern, instead waiting to try and force him to break the pattern first, then you not only run the risk of nothing changing, you risk letting the relationship run itself into the ground.

It doesn't take two people to initiate change in a relationship; it takes one. And it only takes one person to make you happier – you. Here's the thing, you can ask and wish and cajole and pout till the cows come home, but none of those are actions. Until you change your behaviour for the better you're not controlling how your life will change for the better.

If you keep listening to your ego while it says everyone around you should be tending to your needs you're ignoring the fact that with a few simple modifications you'll tend to your deepest needs yourself. Because your ego is the epitome of selfishness it doesn't understand that when you invest time and effort into someone else you get it back in spades.

Your ego is the very opposite of happiness and evolution, so when you feel it flare up don't feed the fire. Let it have its flash, and then move on and do something that'll not only reward your partner, but ultimately you too.

CHAPTER 17

Advice From a Man

I didn't get this smart about relationships because mine was always perfect, and I didn't get this smart about men without help. My relationship hung by a wire at times, and the last time that happened I got some advice from a man that amounted to giving CPR to our marriage. Here it is:

Don't underestimate the power of a grand gesture – As shocking as this may sound, men value grand gestures just as much as women do. I know! I thought we were the only ones who required them but apparently men, being as emotional as we are, can feel delicate too.

Hubby and I were going through a really hard time, and both of us were asking ourselves if we could go on together. One thing was certain though. We couldn't keep going on like this. For a while I didn't even know if I wanted to stay in the relationship, and it took me some time to finally realize that yes, I did. But where should I go from here? How could I begin repairing all the damage that had been done?

Fortunately, I had a man in my life who could not only give

me the male perspective my female brain couldn't generate, but the view around my own ego that I desperately needed.

"He needs a grand gesture," he told me, and, I'll be honest, those words surprised the heck out of me. I mean, weren't grand gestures reserved for women? But I swallowed my bias and drove straight to my husband's shop to tell him that I still loved him and wanted to give our relationship a chance to survive.

And although that cracked the ice a bit, there was still a considerable amount of hurt hanging in the air between us. This made me uber sensitive, and when I called him at work one day and got a terse tone of voice I immediately got defensive. Which leads me to my next lesson from a man.

Don't sweat his moments – "Ignore that," my friend said. "He's stressed out (he was, he was planning a move from his current location to a bigger workshop) and you have to not take his tone personally. That's not about you. Don't make a big deal about it."

So I let the indignant flaring of my ego pass, and with that, so did the moment. And later when we spoke again his tone had softened, and I was glad I hadn't turned that minute into days of anger.

So okay, there I was putting put my heart on my sleeve, re-stating my commitment to making our relationship work and tossing my ego aside for the sake of peace. Now what? Sure, I felt we were a tiny bit closer to avoiding divorce but I felt… lonely. Un-tended to.

What about me?

I complained to my friend. "Go bring him meals," he said, and I instantly bristled. WTF? Why should I keep putting myself out for him without getting anything in return? After a heated exchange (seriously, I was pissed) I finally conceded to giving it a try. And because of the success I experienced this is where the philosophy of putting my man's needs before mine in order to be happier was born.

Here's what happened.

I started bringing him food at his workshop and asking if there was anything I could do to help him out, a tactic I chose knowing his love language was acts of service. And although it didn't happen immediately I have to say the outcome of making a conscious effort to recognize his needs while showing sensitivity to his limitations has paid off tremendously. I find myself saying things like "I'm so happy, baby. Thank you for all the little things and big things you do for me. You do a lot, and I really appreciate it."

It took a man to teach me how to bring another man back from the edge of the abyss, but the lessons he taught me saved our marriage. My husband became my best friend and made an effort to tune into what I needed, making great efforts to make me feel happy and special.

And here's what I learned in all this. We don't always have a choice in how we feel, feelings happen and sometimes we're just along for the ride, but we have a choice in how we behave, and there's always room for something better.

CHAPTER 18

Don't Wish for What You Already Have

S o I was listening to the radio the other day, and CBC was featuring experts talking about the importance of using your vacation days and taking breaks from work. Apparently, it's not only healthy to give your mind a break from taking on the same tasks day in and day out, but you actually come back more productive when you do so.

But here was the kicker. Studies found that most people didn't use up all their vacation time, but when questioned these same folks said they wanted more vacations. Seems kind of crazy, doesn't it? But that's the mentality we have – we wish for something that's already accessible to us while ignoring the fact that we're unhappy because we're failing to take advantage of it.

I know where this comes from too. There's a reason why you keep hearing messages meant to be self-empowering: "Look within yourself!" It's part of a cultural revolution seeking to reverse the conditioning we've been bombarded with pretty much our entire lives.

"Buy this and you'll be happier!" is blasted in our direction non-stop, and we start looking at mirrors and store shelves and car dealerships for happiness. You know, exterior sources.

But we already have everything we want, and we even have the time to exercise it. We're just not taking advantage of what we have in our hands because we're too busy looking outward instead of down at our palms.

Which is, I'm sorry, dumb.

Just like working at your job or anything else for that matter, when it comes to your relationship you have the option to take a breather so you can come back re-invigorated and ready to give a heightened level of effort. And that breather, like any vacation, should be focused on what will make you feel happier, lighter, and vitalized.

That could mean signing up for a yoga class, a painting class with other women and copious amounts of vino, or joining a book club or stealing away a night or two a week to a public library for quiet reading time. It could mean a week away on your own or with your best girlfriend. Whatever you feel would give you some space and a breather, you can and you should give yourself that time.

"Oh, but I'll feel so guilty focussing just on myself!" Okay, so maybe you will, but so what? Guilt is a woman thing, its part of our DNA but it doesn't have to be the reason why you don't take care of yourself.

Uh, what? Part of our DNA? Yep! Let me explain.

How many times have you heard a woman say she felt guilty about something? Even googling the words "guilty pleasure" brings up images of women eating something sweet. So why is guilt largely associated to women? Because we feel it much more than men.

So here's the question: Why is it necessary for women to feel a more powerful guilt response than men?

Again, let me take your hand as we zoom back to our ancestral cavemammas to look at how having a heightened sense of guilt helped her maintain our survival. See the concern on her face when she notices her baby's colour is off just a bit? How she feels torn about leaving it alone for too long? How she won't allow it to cry for long because her guilt makes her a creature built for optimal caring?

A woman's guilt was the emotion that made sure we thrived as a species, and because it was the female who tended to stick around the young ones while the males hunted it just made sense that guilt evolved as a key factor in our nurturing, mothering genes.

So yeah, you're going to feel guilty when you take some you time. But ride it out and allow yourself to take the breaks you need to focus on you. As much as it'll help your relationship when you shelve your ego to look after your man and do your part patching things up, it's equally important to shelve your guilt in order to patch up your own wounded soul.

CHAPTER 19

Understanding the 7 Year Itch

"I feel like we're slipping away from each other."

"I'm more interested in other men than I am in mine right now."

"I think my husband is having an affair."

Have you heard of the 7 year itch? Of course you have, but I bet you don't know why it's a natural part of our biological animal. And although experiencing a 7 year itch is a normal part of our makeup, it doesn't have to be what tears us apart.

But first, let me tell you why it happens. See, wayyyyyy back when, survival rates were below what today's norms are. In fact, when we first evolved most of us didn't live much past 40, so producing the strongest baby possible each and every time we made one was crucial. Especially when you take into account the risks that came with childbirth, being efficient when it came to creating offspring was super important.

So while we would *pair bond* during our mating process and subsequent child rearing years, once that kid was old enough to run from predators and recognize food sources we had a drive to seek out another mate strong enough to ensure the survival of the next baby. For males, this meant younger, stronger, more fertile females, and for females this meant a stronger male, regardless of age.

What does this mean for today's couples? Sure, we're far removed from a time where survival was hanging by a thread and the importance of ensuring a strong gene pool has been overtaken by cultural monogamy. Sure, we no longer have to hunt down our own food and live in caves and be dinner on some other animal's plate. But we still have a lot of the instincts our ancestors were programmed with, and acknowledging this gives us an edge when it comes to understanding where certain behaviours come from.

Because when we understand it we can work past it, using our logical minds to effectively circumvent our biological animal instincts.

So here you are (or here he is), looking outside the relationship with interest while the focus you used to have for your partner is dwindling. This doesn't need to spell the disaster you think it does. This is a natural part of our human, biological cycle, and with time and insight it can pass. All it takes is a commitment to waiting it out and maintaining love as a verb for your partner.

Here's the thing – just because one of you has turned your sights outward it doesn't mean action will follow. It can be a momentary curiosity triggered by our brains, and given time that focus can once again be directed back to who is perceived to be the best partner.

If you've got a good man who's working hard to ensure your happiness, your sights will eventually turn back to him. If you yourself are a good woman working hard to ensure his happiness, eventually his sights will turn back to you.

This is a process I call "re-pairing." You are instinctively looking outside of your relationship for the next mate, and when you see that the best one is the one who is still beside you you'll make your new choice your old partner, once again pairing with them for another seven years. You're re-pairing with them!

Personally, I love the double meaning on this word play. On the one hand you're choosing to pair again with your old mate. On the other hand, having a partner looking outside the relationship can feel hurtful, and repairing your relationship in order to maintain it is very healing.

What I want you to take away from this is the fact that it's absolutely normal for either of you to lose focus on your relationship from time to time. It's a biological, instinctual function for our DNA to say, "Hey, it's time to ensure I go on within the strongest context possible." We are monogamous by culture, not by nature, and if you doubt that consider this: We are mammals, and the percentage of mammals worldwide that are instinctively monogamous is three to five percent out of 5,000 species.

"No way, Chantal! We're totally monogamous!" Yep, you might think so, because you've never, not even for a second, looked at another man while in a committed relationship and thought about what it would be like to share a kiss or spend a night with them… right? Because that's the litmus test for a species, including ours.

In a species where the practice is to choose a mate and stick with it forever, interest in a singular mate is hyper-focused. Trust me, if the monogamous swan had moments where it thought "Ooo, that other one's cute" it wouldn't be monogamous because there's nothing holding it back from acting on its desires. No social pressure, no cultural leaders shaking a finger, no judgement.

So it's obvious to me that monogamy is not part of our genetic makeup, given how even in a loving, solid relationship I can still crush on Robert Downey Jr. But I choose to not pursue any other man, instead enjoying a fun moment wondering what it would be like to spend a day with Ironman before turning my love and attention back to making my husband a hot supper on a cold day.

When you understand that monogamy is cultural rather than biological and give allowances for how our natural instincts flow you infuse your relationship with the sort of understanding it needs. Because if you get caught up with fighting over our instincts rather than making space for them and choosing behaviours that overcome, you create a lot of unnecessary fights both with your partner and within yourself.

Don't beat yourself up if your attention gets drawn outwards from time to time. Don't beat him up when he seems distracted by what else is out there. Double down on your intent to stay committed to your relationship, and choose behaviours that'll ensure its survival and give your brain space to run through its courses with an impartial point of view. Don't judge it, don't dwell on it, just behave your way to what you want – a loving, solid, committed relationship.

Understand that looking and considering isn't cheating. It's a function of our species, and it can pass without complications if you choose.

CHAPTER 20

Green Eyed Monsters

J ealousy sucks. There's no better way to put it. It sucks when you're the one feeling it, and it sucks to be a victim of our partner's jealousy.

Now, I'm not talking about light jealousy, the kind that momentarily rears its head when your partner strikes you as particularly hot before going out without you. I consider this blip on the jealous scale as normal. We want to protect our emotional and physical investments, and jealousy is in itself just a fear of loss.

But when jealousy transforms itself into behaviours, then we have a problem.

Checking phones, directing what can or cannot be worn, or attempting to control who someone hangs out with is a level of jealousy that crosses the line into destructive behaviours.

If you or your partner are in this territory that's a huge red flag, and professional help needs to be sought ASAP. Why? Because this is part of a downward spiral into uncontrolled behaviour and emotions, and if you don't get out either through therapy or removing yourself from the situation, then you're crossing over into the danger zone.

If you're the one suffering from this level of intense jealousy and you're constantly spinning through thoughts like "he's cheating" and "I'm not good enough to keep his attention" your self-esteem is taking a major blow. Stop. Find help right now and get your mind back on the right track. This is not a headspace where good decisions can take place, and you need to get your brain back under your control because it's getting away from you.

You might have to take a step back from the relationship so you can redirect your thoughts to what you need emotionally. Yes, your partner may be looking elsewhere, but your intense focus on all his behaviours and your accompanying neurotic conduct is driving a wedge even further between you, pushing him away instead of drawing his love towards you.

He may not even be looking anywhere but your jealousy is creating issues where none lie, which will, guess what? Create the problem you think you've uncovered. Ultimately, he's going to start asking himself, "What's the point? If I'm going to be accused of cheating anyway why am I bothering to be this devoted?"

Out of control jealousy will bite you in the ass either way you look at it. If you're jealously holding on to a man who's actually cheating on you (and concrete proof is needed to know that for sure) then you're being self-destructive. You need to let him go so you can find yourself once more.

If you're behaving in a way that tells a good man "I don't trust your morals and values and love for me" you're going to wear him down. Eventually, he'll want to stop fighting about his ethics and seek a relationship where he's accepted for being devoted instead of constantly questioned and checked up on.

If you're in a relationship where your partner is this jealous, then get out. Now. This is a precursor to violent behaviour, and you are tempting fate to see how far it will go. Let your partner know in no uncertain terms that you will not be in a relationship where you are controlled. Get your own place to live, move in with a friend, go stay with Mom. Do whatever you need to get some physical distance between you and this man before things escalate.

Let him know that reconciliation is possible only after he gets help for his emotions and behaviours. If he never chooses to after you leave he never would have while you were together, and things could have gotten far worse because nothing would have had a positive effect on his state of mind.

Your number one commitment should always be your own safety and state of mind. In that order.

So be sure you're safe and not in a controlling relationship, and be sure your state of mind is being positively affected by both you and your partner's behaviour, not dragged into a dark place by either of your thoughts spinning out of control.

CHAPTER 21

Why Are Guys Hanging Around Committed Women?

There's a little something in the animal world called "waiting for mating opportunities." It's how a species manages to interject cunning genetic traits alongside strong ones.

Basically, when it comes to the mating process the female of the species picks a male that shows the kind of traits that best ensure the survival of the young. The males with the ability to beat every opponent in a showdown display the greatest strengths and win the most mating opportunities, but while those same males are off procuring resources cunning males will sidle up to females, waiting for a moment where her hormones have her seeking what's available.

It's the same with us.

Most men will agree that having a "purely platonic" friendship with a woman without any thought of becoming sexual intruding into their minds and motivations is pretty much non-existent. Yes, they'll tell you they just want to be friends and their intent is to just be there for you, but almost

100% of the time their friendship has an underlying intent, even if it's subconscious – to be the arms you fall into when no one else is around.

It's not always a devious thing. It's a subconscious, normal occurrence in our species, and using your logical brain to give this phenomena some perspective will get you far.

Being aware of this means you can avoid being distracted by one of those circling males and creating unnecessary drama in your relationship.

Look, I know that relationships are hard. I know that sometimes even when you're with someone that you have no doubt loves you, you feel lonely. Misunderstood. And sometimes you just miss that spark that used to bring you and your partner together with tenderness and passion. And during those times it's nice to be distracted from a relationship that feels cheerless and troubled.

These men make you feel new and shiny again, like you're seen in a light that stopped shinning on you long ago. You miss that initial rush that happens in the first stages of a relationship, where all your best qualities are bright and enigmatic. You feel like you're making someone's heart skip a beat, which in turn makes your own heart feel thrilled. It's nice to feel like all your little details are appreciated and like someone can't wait to spend a minute of their day with you.

Shiny and new equals fun, and sometimes it's been a long time since you've felt like there was any fun in your relationship.

But know that these men are here for the conquest. They're

not the ones who'll stick with you through thick and thin like your partner will. They're looking to be your distraction while the man you're with wants to be your forever. As in the animal kingdom, they'll let the stronger male expend time and energy procuring resources and providing protection and shelter while they swoop in for a good time when no one's around.

Is it okay to allow them to distract you? To a certain extent, I think so. It's okay to lean on these males for a boost of self-esteem, to re-group your thoughts and lift your spirits. Letting someone tell you you're beautiful, intelligent, interesting, and funny when you feel like your partner sees none of that in you is okay, but letting it progress into a romantic relationship is playing with fire.

You could get pulled from a deeply committed and loving, albeit troubled, relationship into something purely shallow, and that could ultimately leave you with absolutely nothing but a nasty split up and a fun-fun buddy who's gone off looking for his next conquest. You've lost the man willing to work through issues with you for someone wanting nothing more than an easy good time.

Recognize distractions when they pop up. Be wary of men on your periphery paying lots of complimentary attention to you. Enjoy the attention, but don't let it interfere with your ultimate goal – to be with a man with whom you can look back on your collective history with and say, "We have our battle scars, but we've won the war and now we're looking at a beautiful future together."

The man you're going to grow old with is the man who's going to fight alongside you when it comes to creating a wonderful, functional relationship. Getting there is possible but not when you put another man between the two of you. Keep your eyes wide open and use your logical brain, and you'll make it through the tough times without adding another issue to work through.

CHAPTER 22

Why do Men Cheat?

Because the other woman made him feel better about himself.

It's that simple.

She said the things that made him feel validated and seen. She touched his arm and made him feel desirable. She laughed at his jokes and showed gratitude when he gave her something, making him feel smart and appreciated. She elevated his self-esteem.

Be that woman, and the likelihood that your man will cheat on you is greatly reduced. Let another woman fill that role while you angrily knock him down every chance you get and…. Well.

I know that when times get rough hurt and its by-product, anger, get knocked back and forth like a tennis ball at a US Open tournament. Words sting, as do inactions. You stop saying nice things to each other, you stop looking for small ways to care for and boost one another, and both of you end up getting dragged lower and lower mentally and emotionally.

This leaves you both vulnerable to people on the outskirts of your relationship who may be looking for an in, or both of you seeking validation elsewhere because it's not happening at home. Dangerous times indeed.

But while this may be where you are now, it's a completely reversible situation. Hang in there, and I'll show you how.

CHAPTER 23

The Bitch Method Never Works

The Bitch Method – A withholding of love, affection, and words of appreciation in an attempt to train your man to incorporate specific behaviours.

I've not only seen this time and again in relationships, I've done it myself. "Sure, he did this thing for me, but I'm still mad about that other thing he didn't do. So I'm going to show minimal acknowledgement for this thing so he doesn't forget how much he's in the dog house for that other thing."

Have you done that? If not you can skip this chapter, but if yes you'd be wise to pay attention because what you do from this moment on can be the beginning of the 180 change in behaviour you're looking for from your partner.

See, here's the thing about the Bitch Method: It ignores the fact that men build on each success, no matter how small. So when you eliminate success altogether he's got nothing to build on, and you're left in the same place over and over. Disappointed in what you're getting from him in your relationship.

If there's one thing I've learned about men, it's that you won't get what you want if you try to force it from them with anger. But you'll get everything when you drop your anger and frustration and give them what they're looking for when they do something, anything, for you.

Withholding gratitude and appreciation, even for "doing their job" like taking out the garbage or picking up the kids, is one less opportunity you give them to want to do something bigger and better for you later on. Your displays of positive acknowledgement are bricks you choose to add, or not add, to building the house you want to live in together. Put the brick up, and you've made the house slightly bigger, better, and stronger. Don't put the brick up, and you're in the same place as before – vulnerable to the elements.

Each "Thank you, I appreciate that" is added to the last, and it's not long before you build a big, beautiful, strong house.

Or not. It's always your choice.

"But I shouldn't have to thank him! He should be doing these things because it's his job." So? Sure, you show up to work every day or get up with the kids every morning because you should, but isn't it nice when your boss calls you into the office just to say your efforts are being recognized, and isn't it great when someone compliments how well behaved your kids are and say you're a good mom? We thrive when we're seen and complimented on our efforts, and it's the same for men.

Did you know that statistically speaking men are more comfortable being single than women are? This is because their lizard brain tells them that once a female is chosen as a mate everything that's required of them is increased. More effort is needed to provide adequate resources like food and shelter, and they're prepared to rise up to the challenge and be good mates and fathers. But when they make that effort to rise only to be met with negativity and lack of acknowledgement there's a spinning that takes place in their heads. "What am I doing all this for?"

There isn't a woman I've worked with who hasn't seen a big turnaround in a man's behaviour simply by shelving her negative emotions and infusing gratitude for everything, big or small. Tossing aside the Bitch Method and replacing it with gratitude has always paid off huge for my clients, each and every time. And fast.

Look, men are waiting for this and the moment it happens they perk up like a dog's ears when you say the word "treat." See, relationships fail when we disregard the impact even the smallest gestures have, whether it's yours and his. Treat his like they don't matter, and you'll train him to stop trying. Treat yours like they don't matter, and he'll stop trying to win them.

Lose, lose.

Everything counts in a relationship. Everything. Nothing is too big or too small to pay attention to. Trying to get him to do something bigger by ignoring his smaller efforts is like trying to fit a roof over thin air. You've got to lay those bricks, one by one, before you have four walls solid enough to put that big roof on.

CHAPTER 24

Why Isn't He Doing What I Need?

Here's my question back at you: Are you letting him know you need him? I don't mean need him to take out the garbage, walk the dogs, bring the kids to school, or wipe the counter after making toast. I mean, are you letting him know that you need him emotionally too?

Men don't want to take care of you because it's required of them, they want to take care of you because you've created a space in your life that they feel only they can fit into. A maid or personal assistant could do all those hundreds of little things you're expecting of him, but if you can't assign him the job of being your emotional guardian then what's his motivation to be The Man In Your Life? You know, the one who takes care of you and does his best to ensure your happiness?

If his job description doesn't include putting his arms around you and making everything okay then he feels like there's an emotional aspect missing from your relationship, and all he's there for is assistance with duties. How mundane.

It's not a burden to him to be what you need emotionally. In fact, it lays the groundwork for him to want to be what you need as a helper and father. But he has to first know without a doubt that you've chosen him to be the man in your life, and unless he can be your supportive, emotional shoulder to lean on all the rest lacks deeper meaning to him. Yes, he'll do his household responsibilities, but what's missing is the feeling of partnership, of kinship, of you two against the world as a united front taking care of business.

He wants to be what you need, but you have to let down your walls and actually need him in a way that's more than just practical. Men are happy to go the extra mile for a woman, but they want to work hard for the one they care about, not just anyone. And how does a man come about caring for a woman? They care for the woman they know cares for them.

Doing little things for him like bringing a coffee or buying him gloves because you know he lost his count as much as any of the big things you could do. Every time you do something that makes his brain click on the "she cares for me" button, motivation is created within him. And the present moment is always the perfect time to forget the past and begin a new way of being.

And know that men aren't built like women. They're as different inside their skulls as they are outside their bodies. Don't expect them to pick up on the fine details and automatically do them. It's not in their DNA to notice little things like we are, nor are they as capable at multitasking as us, but they do want to make us happy. Especially when we start showing gratitude for what they do. So be specific about what you want, be calm about the timeframe, and show happiness when they get any job done. You'll notice an escalation in his desires to put your needs in his priority box.

CHAPTER 25

Create Emotional Closeness

A lasting relationship depends on repeated infusions of warm fuzzies flowing back and forth between the two of you. But how do you bring back that loving feeling? How do you start anew if you feel you can't even remember what that was like?

Sometimes the hardest battle we'll have with our man is creating an emotional closeness, especially if there's been a lot of fighting going on. Usually for us this stems from a feeling of not being heard and comforted, and the angst that creates makes us thorny as hell. It's hard feeling like we're talking to a brick wall, but I'm going to teach you how to tear that sucker down and get the comforting ball rolling.

Lucky for you, men with kind and generous souls are forgiving and willing to move on when the proper healing techniques are applied. The best predictor of future behaviour is past behaviour, and the moment you begin to pave a new road they're right alongside you, paving away. Yes, it'll take some time before they truly trust that you've created a new way of being, but once you're able to point to the last few months and say, "Look baby, I've consistently changed the way I'm behaving for the past three, four, five, six months," their brains start to relax and they begin to really understand that you're transitioning together.

Patience is key here, so be sure you're meditating regularly. This will keep you from personalizing his actions and reactions and give you the ability to simply create a new space and wait for him to catch up.

Now what you're going to do is show him that you need his loving support and teach him how to offer that in a way that feels right for you, and in those moments create an opportunity to feel close and loving with each other again.

Those scenarios where you feel frustrated with what's going on with your day and need a good verbal dumping followed by a hug? Doesn't it just piss you off to no end when you simply want to vent and he keeps coming back at you with what you should have been doing differently? And don't you get angry because he's not getting what you need and end up walking away sans hug, instead packing another pocket full of anger and frustration directed at him because you weren't diffused the way you needed?

What if you could change that? You can, and here's how.

First, you have to begin your story by telling him exactly how you want things to go. "I had such a shitty thing happen today baby, I need to vent about it. Can you listen without saying anything so I can just get it out, and then put your arms around me and tell me everything is going to be okay?"

Believe me, you'll have never seen a man say yes so quickly.

Tell him your story, and if he interrupts gently say, "Baby, I just need you to listen for a bit cause I just have to say it to get it out, then I need you to put your arms around me and tell me everything is going to be okay."

Then, the moment you're done venting your story look him in the eye and say, "Okay, I need you to put your arms around me now and tell me everything is going to be okay."

It might sound like I'm being repetitive here, but that's the level of clarity you need with your man. The first time will likely be the hardest to get through simply because in a way it's your training moment, but he'll catch on quickly and get better at it as time goes on.

Doing this creates a win win scenario for both of you. You, because you get to do the venting you need and have it followed up with the comforting hug that makes everything feel better. And it's a win for him because he gets to feel like he actually helped you and is The Man Of The Hour for making everything better.

And of course, there's the oxytocin. This beautiful, exhilarating chemical is produced when physical touch is exchanged, and its effects are heart-warming, calming, and best of all, memory erasing. So with that hug not only are you making each other feel warm and fuzzy, you're also erasing from your mind the intensity of negative emotions you were suffering before you let your man help you through this tough time.

Clarity is so key to having an incredible relationship. You can't expect your man to come home, notice you're off center, and do all the right things to make you feel good again. Clearly laying out what you need and including him in the solution is such a beautiful way to have a partnership with your man, and he'll absolutely love this.

"Oh no! I can't just tell him to do this!" Why not? Is pride getting in your way? Then pride is getting in your way of love, plain and simple.

Listen, pride is a normal emotion. If we didn't have a high level of pride woven into our DNA what would be our emotional reward when the babies we gave birth to became little people who accomplished things on their own after we taught them how? Pride is super functional when it comes to raising self-sufficient human beings, and a functional motivation tool for accomplishing more ourselves. But when pride blocks you from communicating your needs it becomes dysfunctional, and you need to kick that emotion to the curb.

"Oh, but I feel so uncomfortable saying those things." Do it anyway. There's no tape over your mouth, your lips aren't sewn shut, your tongue isn't glued to the roof of your mouth. You have every capability of getting the words out, so do it despite the nagging voice in your head telling you that doing so is a sign of weakness.

Voicing your needs takes courage. Staying silent and fuming that you're not getting what you need from your partner requires nothing more than ego, and ego is the weakest part of your psyche.

Break the pattern of letting your ego tell you what to do. Take control of your state of mind and take control of how your needs will be met. It's in your power to change the course of your relationship, but giving your power to your ego is the most destructive, unproductive thing you can possibly choose.

Choose communication, not ego. Choose love, not ego. Choose understanding and patience, not ego. It's either/or, but it's always up to you.

CHAPTER 26

Stop Fighting Over Little Things

I'm going to tell you about a technique that pretty much halted 99% of the fights between my husband and me. I call it Balancing, and it's ridiculously simple.

There's a type of scale called the classic weighing balance, where you have two pans on either side of a center beam. I mentioned earlier how relationships fail because we underestimate the power our little acts of caring will have on our partner. The other reason relationships fail is because we attribute too much angst to all the little things we feel our partner is not doing.

When our amygdala is over functioning we let a lot of small things drive us crazy, and they build up until we go nuclear. But what if you could diffuse all those small things, one by one, like a bomb crew going around and unplugging the red wires before something blows up?

Think about that balancing scale again. See how that little thing he forgot to do is weighing one side down? Now, what I want you to do is take a moment and put something of yours on the other side. What did you forget to do?

It's not fair to take a magnifying glass to his faults without taking a peek at yours too, and failing to do so will tear your relationship apart bit by bit, enacting that death by a thousand cuts and bleeding the life out of it till it drains dry. This isn't what you want, and balancing his imperfections with yours is exactly how you'll stop that.

And do you know what? Balancing feels great! That buildup of anger was instantly dissolved when I let my mind stack my neglecting to pick up dog poop alongside his not getting bread on the way home.

It's okay for you to not be perfect, and it's okay for him to not be perfect too. Balancing is a great way to acknowledge that both of you are going to drop the ball from time to time, and that both of you will let the moment pass without letting it become something larger than life.

But what if you feel like you're pulling more than your share of the load around the house? Are you paying the majority of the expenses plus doing the majority of the household chores? Division of labour can be a huge fighting point in a relationship. It needs to feel balanced. Otherwise, resentment can grow to catastrophic levels. So how do you ensure responsibilities are balanced out?

First, be sure you're clearly looking at who's paying what, and who's doing what. You might feel things are unfair, but are you absolutely clear about what's happening or are you a little blinded by negative emotions? That happens, so taking some time to take stock is important because should you need to renegotiate something you have facts on your side, not opinions.

Take a month and start writing down who pays what and who does what. At the end of thirty days tally up the dollar amounts and hours of labour and see how they stack up. You might be surprised and ultimately soothed by that level of clarity.

But if at the end of a month of putting facts down on paper you see that you're pulling your weight and his too, then it's time to sit down and have a conversation. Show him what you've found and let him know: "I don't feel it's fair that I'm doing this much financially and physically. Let's find a way where this becomes more equal."

Don't make it a fight, and stick to the words, "I don't feel it's fair." Staying calm will force him to maintain focus on the issue at hand. Ask him what he feels the solution should be, and let him come up with something that works for the both of you. Making him part of the process empowers him to act and makes him feel less like a child who's being told what to do. And as we all know, men hate being told what to do.

Write down the solutions as he comes up with them, and put them on the fridge. Putting his words in writing reminds him that he's the one who created that clarity, and putting it where he'll see it reminds him that he gave himself responsibilities. Then let it go for another thirty days, keeping track of money and chores again. If it hasn't balanced by the fourth week then it's time to have another talk. Should he consistently show an unwillingness to step up and have an equitable relationship you might be with a guy and not a man. And remember, the best predictor of future behaviour is past behaviour. Is this what you want for the rest of your life?

CHAPTER 27

What a Man Wants

Trying to understand how men think using our female brain is like trying to "get" the colour red when you've been blind since birth. We are so different in the way we think and function, and we'll never truly understand each other. But what we can do is understand each other's needs and accommodate them.

Think of it this way. As an adult you have absolutely no recollection of what it's like to be a baby, but if I put one in your arms right now and it starts to cry what are you going to do? Get upset because it obviously needs something, or start looking for what needs tending to so you can bring that baby back to a happy place as soon as possible?

It's the same with men. They'll have routine needs that you can plug into and accommodate that'll help them be happier day to day. But instead of offering a bottle or checking for a dirty diaper you can be accepting and understanding of their main differences and make allowances for their needs.

There are two things we can learn about men that will give them a sense of much needed understanding. Their need for space and their need for quiet.

First, space. Coded into their DNA is a desire to go forth and roam, and it was this drive that helped them become proficient hunters and bring back enough food for their family. Go out, come back. Go out, come back. This back and forth is as natural to them as breathing, and their brain naturally flows in and out of our presence like this.

What does this mean in your relationship? Well, you'll notice from time to time that he seems distant and pre-occupied. For women who aren't aware of the flux and flow of a man's brain this can seem alarming, but fear not! It just means his brain has gone a-huntin' and will be back with more. In this case, instead of more food it'll be more emotion and more connection.

But you have to let them go mentally, so you can reap the rewards of their strengthening commitment. That means not freaking out when they seem far away and disconnected, instead just being patient and waiting until it's obvious they've plugged back in. You'll notice their return when they become more affectionate and attentive to your needs, seeking that happiness in your eyes that they're programmed to desire.

What do you do in the meantime? Meditate! Maintaining a shrunken amygdala means you don't take these moments personally, overreacting and becoming clingy in an attempt to draw them back in. Look after yourself and your personal desires by asking yourself "What do I want?" and giving yourself permission to take care of you.

And when he comes back looking for attention welcome him with open arms. Give him all the love and affection and kisses he's seeking. He might have been sharing a house with you all along, but mentally he took a hiatus and he misses you now. This is the time where you help him build his love and devotion, before he sets off mentally again looking for how he can feed and fortify his family.

Another thing men appreciate is a quiet presence. It's hard to grasp, but they do this thing called "nothing" in their heads. Unbelievable. They actually have moments where nothing is going on in their minds and they just kind of rest there. I mean, can you imagine? Me neither.

But they do, and they need us to let them do that. Which means believing them when we ask, "What are you thinking?" and they reply, "Nothing." It also means being able to sit quietly beside them.

Now I know how hard that can be, trust me. We women process 20,000 words per day, so it's natural for us to want to talk, but men only process about 5,000 words a day. This is why I always say women need their girl group. Nobody can naturally understand and accommodate us like another woman can.

Being able to sit silently yet lovingly beside our men is our gift to them, because letting a man be who he is without demanding he be more like us is one of the most generous things we can do. He'll appreciate being able to be himself without having to be plugged in at every moment. Letting his brain rest in our presence makes them much happier to be around us too, and associating a sense of peace, relaxation, and easy companionship to us strengthens his feelings, making it easier for him to step up and accommodate us when we need it.

Another thing I do is teach women how to communicate with men so they're heard. A trick to remember here is the art of few words. See, because their brains process a quarter of the words we do using too many to get a message across only complicates what we're saying.

Consider this: "I need you to take out the garbage tonight, cause I dumped some old leftovers and I don't want it to smell by tomorrow morning. And you know how much I hate getting up and having to deal with a stinky kitchen."

Compared to this: "Hey, baby, can you take out the garbage tonight? Thanks, my love!"

For them, it's the difference between "please take care of this for me" and '"Wa wa, wawa, wa wa wa." Our brains are functioning at a faster, more frantic pace than theirs. Simplifying our behaviours around them makes them feel more at home than asking them to become as complicated as we are, and for the sake of harmony finding it within us to become quieter and more to the point is working *with* their brains, instead of against it.

Ultimately, your partner will feel like you get them like no other woman can. Which is a sweet place to be seen from.

Step 3 – Overcoming Fear

Sometimes the biggest liar is inside your own head.

CHAPTER 28

Fear Is a Drunk Driver

There's a lot to be afraid of in a relationship. What if my efforts don't pay off? What's going to happen down the road? What if I'm never happy with this person? What if I get everything right, only to lose the best thing I've ever created to some terrible accident?

What if?

Every scenario associated to fear is just that, a scenario. Fear is something you feel today about what could happen tomorrow, but because we've been gifted with imagination we've also been cursed with the ability to mentally create a reality that scares the crap out of us. You can thank mainstream media for further helping that aspect of our brains along by constantly triggering our fear reactions and supersizing our amygdalas.

Fear is a huge part of our existence, having been embedded in our DNA in order to keep us alive. Fear kept us from approaching a lion's den, from leaning too far over the edge of a cliff, from venturing too far from the fire into the depths of a dark night when predators liked to come a-creeping.

We used to use fear as a functioning tool for survival, but now it's time to fight back. It's time to live with courage, to take control of our existence instead of letting fear control our lives. It's time to take a stand against our own imaginations and begin to foresee a better future, one in which we're happy instead of making decisions focused solely on trying to not shit our pants.

In today's safe world constantly avoiding the things that scare us is the definition of merely existing. But boldly moving forward despite the tendrils of fear that can wrap around our hearts is the definition of living life to its fullest.

Look, I'm not saying you're going to stop feeling fear. I'm saying you don't need to listen to it. Fear is a feeling, but what you choose to do is your reaction to fear. If you're constantly basing your choices on avoidance rather than desired outcomes, guess what? You're always pinging back and forth from one negative feeling to another, always living in fear, always being reactive, and never proactively taking the helm of your existence and creating the life you want.

So let's take a moment so I can ask you two very important questions. What do you want, and what are you afraid of? Because these are the questions that will unlock the rest of your life. These are the questions that can open the gates to everything good.

What do you want? A great relationship that feels harmonious, satisfying, engaging, filled with love and generosity. Right? What else? If you made a list it would certainly be filled with all your hopes and dreams. With light, love, happiness, fulfillment, and joy.

What are you afraid of? What's this list filled with? Shattered dreams, broken emotions, deathbed wishes? Some of those fears are ghosts of the past looming before you, shreds of prior experiences shadowing your future and filling your head and heart with dread.

All those fears are normal, and I certainly won't tell you they're not valid. But here's the thing: If you're constantly seeking to avoid fear you're never reaching the other side, instead staying on this safe yet unsatisfying side of the road. See, this side is super familiar, isn't it? And we seek what's familiar, even if it's bad for us. Familiar is comforting in its predictability even if what's predictable is more dysfunction. Strange but true.

Fear of the unknown is normal for us, because it takes us beyond our norms. Do you want to hear something so weird I never thought I'd say? Having my own relationship become super awesome was scary. It was strange and unfamiliar territory because I'd never had a relationship with anyone become so full of love and void of conflict. For a while, every month I'd feel afraid that we would have a big blow out fight and the peace that had reigned for the past while would dissolve into our old, familiar pattern of discord.

Regardless of what's happening in your life, whether it's good or bad, fear will pop up. Count on it. But fear isn't something we should trust. Fear isn't something we should put in the driver's seat of our lives while we sit beside it saying, "Okay, buddy, take me home."

Because if you let fear drive the car it's always going to drive down the same familiar roads. And hey, if you're happy then that's fine. But if you're not then you've got to take a new road, and that means facing fear and plowing through it. It means looking fear in the face and saying, "Look, you're just a feeling, a fog. You're not solid, and there's no reason why I should let you block my path. You're wisps, not bricks, and I've got the courage to get on the other side of you and see what's there."

I know you've faced fear before and overcome it. That first time you stepped off a diving board, got behind the wheel of a car, signed your first loan, or walked through a door on your first day of work were you looking your fear in the face and saying, "Not today. I've got shit to do." You're familiar with fear, and you're adept at overcoming it, but sometimes it freezes you, especially when it comes to matters of the heart.

And that's okay. For a moment. Of course you want to protect yourself, I get that. But being so guarded, so cautious, so frozen in space and time that it interferes with where you really want to go won't work for you, and you've got to step off that board one more time. Walk through that door for the sake of your future heart and its fulfillment.

Come, dear reader. You've got this.

CHAPTER 29

The Dysfunctional Relationship Between Fear, Ego, and You

One day fear met ego, and they both said, "Wow! This is a match made in heaven! Let's get married." Fear loved to feed and defend ego, keeping it fat and safe. And ego always did a great job of flattering fear, constantly validating it and being sure to tell it the words it wanted to hear all day, every day. "You're right, honey! In fact, you are never, ever wrong."

And so they got married and lived happily ever after, wreaking havoc on your life.

Haven't you noticed that feeling of fear every time you start to consider your role in any of the fights you have with your partner? How the moment he points out your imperfections you feel defensive, your mind instantly screaming, "He can't possibly be right about how wrong I am!" How the thought of being the first to say "I'm sorry" fills you with dread? Cause there's no way you're more wrong than him, and he better say sorry first.

That's your fear and ego holding hands and skipping merrily through your thoughts. And look, that's not pixie dust they're spreading everywhere. It's dried, powdered crapola.

But here's the thing, you have a right to disagree with both of them. And aren't you tired of the cycle of negative feelings being exchanged between you and your loved ones because you keep letting fear and ego's theories rule your decisions?

When it comes to creating a relationship that works in your favour you've got to start eliminating what isn't working for you, and that means realizing that those two jerks are really getting in your way. They say things that aren't true because they want to stay right where they are, living in that plush, cushy space you've given them inside your mind. They know if you start ignoring them they'll grow smaller and smaller, their significance will shrink, and along with that their star power will fade until all they become are afterthoughts.

And so they realize that there's strength in numbers, and they hope that by creating an alliance they appear to be too strong for little ol' you to push out of the way. They puff themselves out, whisper sweet nothings in your ear and try to fill you up with their greatness, hoping you won't realize you really don't need them to feel good about yourself after all.

They make you choke on the words and actions that would heal your relationships and distract you from the power they hold over you. See, they don't want you to have love for anything else because they feed on your attention and are selfish, wanting it all for themselves. Don't love him, love us.

Don't listen to him, listen to us. Don't feed him with your consideration, feed us. Don't validate him, validate us. Don't give him a safe place to come to at the end of the day, give us that safe place.

And so you do, over and over, and in the end you're left standing all alone, just you and them. "It's okay," they whisper in your ear, "we'll never ever leave you. See, you were right all along. Nobody can love you like we can. Nobody cares about you as much as we do."

How do you recognize this nasty couple living inside you? They exist in the flush, the rush of heated emotions exploding through your torso and engulfing your brain whenever someone dares point a finger in your direction saying, "Hey! You've been playing a part in this negativity too."

See, introspection and courage are their worst enemies. If you looked deep within yourself, acknowledged your flaws, and began to speak from love instead of from defensiveness, where would they go? They can't survive in the sort of environment where courage reigns and understanding and compassion comes first.

But what do you want? Do you want to live alone with fear and ego? Because I guarantee they'll drive away everything you love and desire. All your dreams will lie on the other side of fear, and all the love you want will be blocked by ego. Or do you want close, lasting, intimate love and the ability to reach for any star you seek? If you do, you need to see and overcome your limitations, and have the balls to be humble and openly honest.

You might not know this yet, but breaking up with fear and ego is like getting rid of the worst best friends you've ever had. You feel like they've had your back all along, but in fact their advice has always been self centered, intent on keeping you all to themselves no matter what the cost. The moment you kick them out of your life you're opening a ton of new doors, giving yourself an opportunity to connect with what you really want.

CHAPTER 30

See the Monsters, Fight the Monsters

Ever watch one of those movies where a priest is performing an exorcist on someone and insists the demon name itself so he can drive it out? There's something about naming a fear that begins the process of incapacitating it.

With understanding comes compassion, and once you really get the gist of what you're afraid of you can give yourself the grace you need to get through it. Fear of rejection, fear of abandonment, fear of appearing foolish, fear of failing. These are all very common fears in a relationship, but when you face them head on and call them out you'll know just what to do to shoo those demons away.

Facing and owning your fears is the first step to overcoming them because when you always pin the source as "out there" you disempower yourself to deal with them. If all your fears are his fault and you can't change him, then you're doomed to live with them for as long as you live with him. And the next guy. And the one after that.

But if your fears are yours to own and therefore control then you're fully able to dismantle them. Which is good, right? Because now that means you can move past them in this relationship, and doing so might create the healing space you so desperately need. That means you won't end up with a new guy feeling fearful all over again.

Which means... The buck stops here.

Here is where you take a stand, plant your feet firmly, and say, "I don't care how scary you look, with your wild hair and crazy voice and 360 spinning head while you're crawling on the ceiling. I'm stronger than you, I'm louder than you, and no matter what I'm not giving in to you. By the power of my newfound courage, I compel you to stop tainting my relationships with your BS."

Your fears come from a lot of different sources, and they'll surface in a multitude of ways. The type of environment you grew up in can create fears that you'll end up just like your parents. Your relationship history can make you afraid you'll get burnt once again. And your own insecurities can make you terrified of never being loved and accepted for who you are.

Name it. Face it. Overcome it.

"Yeah, but it's not that easy. These fears run deeeeeeeep, and I've been carrying them with me all my life!"

Listen, it's so much easier than you think. You just don't know that yet because you've never really fought fear the way I'm teaching you. When in your life have you ever made a concerted effort to shrink the fight or flight system in your brain? I promise you, if you listen to what I say and do the exercises in this book your fears will shrink faster than you've ever imagined. All you need to do is give yourself a chance.

The first fear I want you to overcome is the one about things not working out. No matter what the outcome have faith that it'll be the right one for you. Before my hubby and I got married he sometimes tried to tell me that I'd be lost without him. Now, I certainly had a ton of fears and insecurities when it came to our relationship, but the one thing I already had confidence in was my own ability to choose a path and blaze my way to success with or without a man by my side.

This too has to be your first stand. Look at everything you've accomplished so far. Look at how far you've come. Look at how amazing you are. Don't ever forget how hard you've worked to be this woman and everything you've fought to create.

Are you having trouble doing this? Then I've got some homework for you before you go any further.

Grab a pen and a piece of paper and write in big bold letters at the top "I Am." You're going to see yourself in all your glory because until you do you have no idea just how powerful you are.

Your I Am statement is the most powerful thing you'll ever say because it clarifies and defines you. If you say "I am weak, I am powerless, I am not in control. I am defined by what he says about me, I am unable to do this" then you can't help but be those things. But if you take a good look at yourself and see past all your insecurities to who you truly are and allow yourself to acknowledge all your amazingness with statements like "I am smart, I am resourceful, I am strong, I am capable, I am ambitious, I am a good mother, I am supportive, I am loving" you build yourself up in the image that is truly you.

Don't let your mind get swamped by negativity. That's a baloney thing to allow. The fact is, our brains are geared to focus on the negative, but you're the one who's at the wheel and you can turn it around any time you want. So get your mind out of the muck and start to look up instead of down.

So sit down and write out fifty "I am" statements. That's right, fifty. Every single one of them has to be positive too. No "I am a couch potato, I am introverted, I am shy." There's nothing wrong with enjoying your couch time and liking your own company, but these need to be bold, strong positive statements.... If you stall at thirty then dig deep. What glowing qualities do your friends say about you? Write them down. What nice things have family members said to you? Write them down.

Do you feel uncomfortable being complimentary about yourself? Screw that. Listen, if you can't bring yourself to see how great you are you'll never accept anyone thinking you're amazing, and you'll always be miserable in your relationships because you'll reject the notion that someone can love everything good about you.

Being afraid of being great is the first fear you have to drive back. Make your list and work at it until you've acknowledged fifty admirable things about yourself, and wrap this image around yourself to use as your shield against anyone who dares bring you down. You're awesome and you're gonna see it, use it, and love it.

Next I want you to face your fear of the future. It's normal to feel uncertain about where your life is going but here's the thing – the future ain't here yet. Which means you're pre-occupying your mind with speculations instead of reality. The reality is, the future is yet to be determined unless you continue doing the same things you've already been doing, in which case it's likely much more predictable. Remember, the definition of insanity is repeating the same behaviours and expecting different results. Change your behaviours and you'll change your future.

So let go of what you're afraid will happen. Focus on what you have power over, which is the present moment and what you're doing with it. Make this a mental exercise every time you find yourself spinning round fears of what could be. "I'm afraid I'm going to be alone, I'm afraid my family is going to split up." Okay, but what's happening right now? You're still together, right? Ground yourself in today, think about what you'll change today, and stay in the moment, because it truly is all that you have. The past is healable, the future is yet to happen, and the present is where the magic takes place. Have faith.

Whatever the outcome, you're going to be okay.

CHAPTER 31

Triggers

Triggers – we all have them. Your brain is filled with neural pathways, and because each one is associated to an experience it's easy for similar experiences to bring us down a dark road. I've had my own to contend with, like being afraid my second marriage would end up like my first every time my husband slept on the couch because in my past this behaviour ultimately ended in divorce.

Grief can be triggered, along with sadness, pain, fear, and insecurity. It's going to happen, but the question is what are you going to do about it? Again, and I can't say this enough, you've got to meditate. Shrinking your fight or flight center will make a huge impact on how much you're affected by, and can move past, all those triggers. It's like your triggers are fires and meditation is the water that'll put them out. If you haven't made a solid decision to meditate yet make this the paragraph that sways you.

Now, assuming you're meditating, how else do you handle your triggers? You have to let the moment pass. Although meditation will greatly reduce the severity and increase your ability to move past them you're still going to feel emotional reactions, and you need to be prepared to deal with that.

Learning to release your emotions in what I call controlled demolitions is your #1 tool, and knowing that your brain will go off and giving yourself permission to cycle through feelings without being reactive is your #2 tool. Remember that there's a difference between what happens in your mind and what you create in your world. One is a mental reaction, and the other is what you actually control, so when you find yourself spinning down a dark alley of past pain triggered by something today, stop. Take a moment and ask yourself a very important question.

What is my reality?

Reality is what's happening right here, right now. Keep it simple because simplicity is the ultimate sophistication. In essence, simple is beautiful, and what's beautiful is what's actually going right, not what might go wrong or what has gone wrong.

Look at this moment. What's good about it? Is your health okay? Do people love you? Do you have a warm place to sleep at night, food to eat, a TV to watch and books to read? Look at what's right and ground yourself into that rightness. Push your brain to find the light instead of allowing it to spin endlessly round and round whatever darkness it brings up.

Look outside and find beauty in the details. Take in how the breeze moves the leaves on a tree, and seek out a blooming flower or sparkling sunlight on snow. Take a second to pet your fur baby and appreciate the love you have for each other. Text a friend and let them know how important their support is to you. There are always a yin and yang to every second of your day, so find the light side even when you feel overwhelmed by darkness.

Your triggers are baggage, luggage you packed long ago and are still carrying around. By its very definition emotional baggage is something that interferes with your development and gets in the way of your future. It sucks your freedom because it anchors you in the past instead of helping you move towards what you really want. Put that down and walk away. The present moment is about your desire to change, making your future something you have control over and can alter in your favour.

Listen, state of mind is either a conscious choice or an unwitting unravelling. Choose wisely.

CHAPTER 32

Insecurity Is an Equal Opportunity Employer

Security. Don't we all want that? It's a quest that drives us nuts, isn't it? We're constantly talking about security versus insecurity and demonizing everything that causes our feelings to tailspin into self-doubt.

But do you know what? Insecurity is such a fundamental part of human nature that even the most beautiful and successful actresses suffer from it. Rarely is anyone immune from this emotion, and neither beauty nor money can fully eradicate the nagging voice in our heads that compare us to unreal standards and whisper, "You're not good enough yet, my love."

Why does this exist in our nature? And what can we do about it because frankly, something needs to be done, right? Because insecurity doesn't only tear you apart from the inside out, it can tear your relationship to shreds too.

Because of insecurity you'll look in the mirror with dislike. You'll dread getting into your car and going to an event. You'll grab your partner's phone or hack into their email.

You'll actively seek what you need to see to validate the fear and loathing that's swirling inside you, confirming that you're right all along to have doubts.

Insecurity is a beast, but you can fight it. Look, I've got your battle axe right here, and it's stamped with the words 'Understanding' and 'Screw That.' Are you ready to swing that sucker and bring your insecurity to its knees? Yes?

Yes!

First, why does this exist in us in the first place? See, the animal in us requires a clear understanding of our positionning in this world. Without firming up a sense of hierarchy and a clear cut knowledge of where we belong in the order of things we're confused, and confusion is counter to survival.

If I walk into a new group and I don't understand and cede to the top dog, my take no prisoners attitude means I'm going to get my head chopped by a stronger foe unwilling to let some ballsy chick upset the order they established. Think about what would happen if everyone in the world walked around with a sense that they have all the confidence needed to run the whole damn show. We'd all be battling it out for top positioning, which means we'd be at war with everyone else. All. The. Time.

In essence, the insecurity woven into our human nature keeps us relatively peaceful amongst ourselves.

Some of us need to feel inferior in order to cede to leadership. It's leadership that gets us from point A to point B, whether it's in a wolf pack, a herd of bison, or an entire country. We need followers as much as we need leaders, and what helps us figure out where we fit into that dynamic is, you guessed it, varying levels of insecurity.

Personally, I don't feel secure enough to lead a whole country, but thank God someone has the guts and will to run for President and Prime Minister. I do, however, feel secure enough to lead a room full of women down a path to feeling more secure, something I didn't feel secure enough to do twenty years ago.

See, insecurity is fluid. It can change along with you, and ultimately you can consider your own goals and desires first, and your level of insecurity second. You can push aside insecurity, just like you can push aside stress and anxiety. You hold the power and key to everything and anything. Hell, you could run for President if you wanted to bad enough, and insecurity would take a back seat if that's how you wanted to roll. Because as much as stuff like this is woven into our DNA, so is free will.

You just gotta want.

So, here's my question to you: Do you want to feel more secure?

Do you want to feel more peaceful about that woman in the mirror? About getting in your car and hitting up that event? About seeing your partners phone on the table and letting it be?

You can. See, insecurity is a moment, a blip in our brains that we can choose to run with or just run in the background along with all those other negative emotions. We can separate our logical minds from the animal instincts that burble with insecurities. We can give it a voice, a reasoning, the validation it clamors for. Or we can recognize it, acknowledge its fundamental nature, and then shrug it off and set our sights on our goals.

Insecurity is going to happen. Over and over, although with meditation you'll experience it less frequently and on a less pervasive scale. You'll notice that this emotion tends to be tied up with anxiety and stress, and by shrinking your amygdala you'll also shrink your capacity to be bogged down with insecurity. Voila!

In the meantime, you have to stop feeding the beast. Every time you feel insecure and you allow it to guide your actions you just gave it a cookie, and in this way it grows and grows.

But every time that emotion whispers directions into your mind and you let the moment pass, instead choosing to do something calming, you take a bite out of it and feed your self-esteem instead. Each decision to not respond to your insecurities swings that hammer and slams the beast on the head. I understand why this bubbles up, and screw that. Wham!

It's a difficult process at first. When we've spent years responding to insecurity instead of analyzing it and turning the other cheek we've created a habit, and as you know, habits can be hard to break. At first anyway.

But I know you've broken at least one before. You're familiar with the process. Resist today, and it'll be easier to resist tomorrow.

I went through a hella huge surge of insecurity during the first few years with my hubby, and I had to learn to get through that so we could have a more peaceful relationship. It's not easy when your lover's ex is living on the same street as him. When he has a password on his phone. When you spend more time apart than together.

My mantra, ultimately, was "I know everything I need to know." Whenever I found my mind racing with insecurities and being infused with directions on how to validate them I had to come up with my own blockade and teach myself how to settle my emotions. Grounding myself in realities instead of letting my imagination race became my go-to approach, and I started becoming my own locker room coach.

"You're awesome! You've got this! Here's your game plan. Look at what he's doing, and duck and weave around the rest."

If I felt insecure about losing him I'd remind myself of my own qualities. I'm smart, intelligent, and funny. If I lost him to someone else I'd be a catch to a man more willing to appreciate me, and frankly, I'd find someone even better because I never left an experience without learning more about myself and improving along the way.

I know everything I need to know about myself.

If I felt insecure about how much he talked to his ex I'd remind myself of his devotion to me. He'd shown me for years, even before we got together, that I was the apple of his eye. He'd had a single minded interest in me long before I was even able to entertain the thought of being with him, and that interest had never wavered. He'd done a lot for me when he was courting me, and he'd done a lot for me once we got together. He'd made me a beneficiary of all his manly qualities and always worked hard to please me.

I know everything I need to know about his devotion and how much he loves me.

If I felt insecure about how much his ex needed his attention or directed sexual innuendos his way I'd remind myself of everything he'd told me about why it hadn't worked between them. I'd see that his kids' happiness was a priority to him and remember that they were the reason she was still in his life. I'd recognize that it was her own insecurities that made her behave in ways that at times seemed disrespectful.

I know everything I need to know about them.

Every time I had an insecurity pop up I'd stop and give myself the coaching I needed to get me through the moment, and each time I gained more strength and security within myself. Listen, your actions can feed your brain or your brain can feed your actions, and every moment gives you an opportunity to decide if you will weaken or strengthen yourself. Give in to insecurity, and you'll forever be insecure.

If you find yourself spinning without proof then maybe it's time to double down on your meditation minutes. It could be you have an overactive amygdala sending distress signals through your system and in an attempt to find a reason you're developing insecurities. Shrink your fight or flight system, and you'll find yourself feeling calmer and more secure, and with that a heightened sense of rationale will take over.

Choose to act securely even in moments where you feel far from it, and you'll start to become stronger and more powerful than your base emotions, carving new paths inside your brain that are reinforced by your behaviours. Eventually, insecurity will be nothing more than a blip.

CHAPTER 33

Sexual Insecurity

The questions that pop up when sex takes a nosedive can torture our minds to no end. Am I less attractive? Will we survive?

I'm here to tell you, it's going to be okay. There are so many reasons for sex to decline in a relationship, and the majority have nothing to do with you. Fatigue, lack of time, lower testosterone levels, and an unwillingness to do it unless you're gonna do it right are all factors that can take chunks out of the number of times you have sex.

It's time to cast doubt aside and roll with the punches.

You may be going through a tough time, and that in itself can make either party unwilling to make a sexual investment right now, but once that's over you need to realize that there are other factors at play too.

See, I used to be a numbers girl. If we weren't having sex a few times a week I'd start to wonder if his interest in me was dwindling and would continue to do so till there was none left and he'd move on to someone else. Scary thoughts, right?

But I learned over time that there are reasons, and solid ones at that, for couples to experience drops in their sex life. And you can't explore them without looking at why they spike in the first place.

First of all, novelty. Newness is so exciting, isn't it? So of course when we first get together there's going to be tons and tons of sex. And then there's our procreation drive, taking over our minds and pushing us to want sex all the time because, subconsciously, we're following a drive to make a baby that'll carry on the existence of the human race.

Then there's the sex we have because of his drive to ensure the proliferation of his DNA code versus another man's. Oh, you didn't hear about that one? It's the reason he's horny for you when you come home after being in the presence of other males. Something in his lizard brain says that while you were away from each other there's a possibility you've procreated with another mate, and not only will your man feel compelled to have sex when he sees you again but his sperm will actually shoot out with more force than usual, forcing it beyond what may have been deposited in you earlier and ensuring his DNA is the one that makes a baby.

Yep. Subconscious jealous sex. It's a male thing as well as a female thing. Might as well enjoy it!

But then, you get accustomed to each other and you find a routine and sex becomes, well, routine.

You get married and there's another drop, since he's not ravishing you when you get home because his lizard brain says, "I can have her anytime I want." I'm quoting my husband on that one, by the way.

Kids or increased responsibilities associated with work or home come into play, and now there's less time and energy to go around.

And then, age creeps up on you both, and with that comes a drop in testosterone levels for both men and women.

Which means it's time to redefine sex. It's time to walk away from the numbers game and create a whole new reason to have sex.

And here it is. Because of love. Or as I like to say, *because Love*, which is, in my mind, the answer to every question in the Universe.

For me, it had to stop being about frequency and come back to connection. I had to evolve my sexuality beyond ego and return to something more emotional, more about sharing and caring, and it had to become more secure.

I had to accept that sex sometimes wasn't going to be weekly anymore, and be okay with long stretches of time now and then. The funny thing was my own sex drive went down before my mind caught up with re-thinking our sexuality, so while I was sometimes shying away from the idea of having sex I was still trapped in feeling insecure at how much less we were having.

But with some research and a little insight I finally settled into feeling more comfortable about why sex can shift throughout our relationships. It's not me, it's him. It's not us, it's me. Whatever the reason, allowing the flux and flow of your sex life to morph and change will separate feelings of insecurity from the process and allow you to embrace wherever you're at. It might be low today, but something later can shift and next thing you know you're in high gear again.

My advice? Just be grateful every time you have sex. Grateful for the opportunity to share something super intimate with each other. Grateful for a chance to experience your body on a whole other level. Grateful for having time to spend together, and for maintaining a bond unlike any other you experience in life.

Each time hubby and I get it on we always say thank you to each other after. *Thank you for taking care of me. Thank you for being my partner. Thank you for taking this time with me to be completely vulnerable, and for holding me after.* Those are the things we're thinking when we say, "Thank you, my baby, I love you."

Life can get complicated. Emotions can get complicated. But sex? We can bring it back to the basics: two people showing each other love and devotion, if only for a moment.

CHAPTER 34

Is It Too Late to Say Sorry?

The short answer? Never.

Why would you want to? Because it clears out the attic, the basement, the closets, and every messy cupboard in the house that your relationship has become. Will you hoard all the times you hurt each other? Or will you take each piece of pain and toss it in a dumpster, one by one?

Cleaning house is the most liberating thing you'll ever do in your relationship, and the process helps you keep it from getting messy again because you become accustomed to keeping garbage from coming in through the front door. Or back door, for that matter.

Turning things around takes time, and choosing to make decisions based on peace instead of ego takes some getting used to. Even after I'd started owning my destructive behaviours I still had some resentment based reactions pop up and cause fights.

The fact is sometimes people are jerks, and what happened in the past resonates long after, ringing in our ears and keeping us from finally clearing our heads. It's this sort of stuff that can come up in our minds when making decisions today, and we can be reactive even years after something was done to wound us. I know I was.

But doing something today in reaction to what hurt me weeks, months, or even years ago only perpetuates those negative feelings, and in that way they never die. He did that, so today when he needs this from me I'm going to retaliate to make him feel bad, because deep down I'm still wounded. And when my reactive behaviour upsets and angers him I'm going to be defensive about his anger and get angry right back. And on and on it goes.

When is it ever going to end?

Someone has to break the cycle. Someone has to say, "Today, we start over. Today I let the past go and I'm not going to let it direct my actions anymore. Today I'm going to bring a brand new me to this relationship and take each day one at a time looking forward only. Today, I'm going to be the one to change things."

It only takes one person to change your life, and that's you. If you want to stop fighting, then stop fighting. If he insists on continuing to fight even after you've been able to point to the last six months and say, "I've stopped, why haven't you?" then he needs help stopping and it's beyond your scope. But what you've gained is the patience and courage to carve a new road for yourself.

It's never too late to say you're sorry for whatever negativity you've taken part in creating, no matter how far in the past it is. Whether it was three years ago or just an hour, saying you're sorry will take that piece of hurt and toss it outside your home.

I'm not promising that it'll happen in one day. Sometimes a piece of hurt is like a huge, heavy piece of furniture, and getting something large and cumbersome out of the house takes time and effort and bunch of pushing and grunting. But you know as well as I do that persistence can achieve just about anything.

Making a decision day by day to own your part, to stay Zen, and to only look forward is what will move things in the direction you want to go. Not expecting him to know how to do this at the pace you're going, instead creating the space and giving him time to step into it will make it all easier. Remember, expectations can be devastating.

You do you, and give him time to do him. He's got to see that day after day, week after week, and yes, month after month you're sticking to your guns. You've got to convince him through your actions that you're serious about change, and consistently model the change you're serious about.

Humans learn more through example than they do by simply being told. You can't tell your man you want him to be apologetic about all the hurt he caused without showing him what that means over and over. Don't give him an opportunity to call you a hypocrite. Learn, become, and in this way you'll teach him what you need and how it's done.

What do you say you're sorry for? Everything. Because don't you want him to be sorry for everything too?

I'm sorry I blamed you for this five years ago. I realize you were doing the best you could.

I'm sorry I did this yesterday. I was feeling resentful of what happened two years ago and I let that resentment colour my actions. That was wrong of me.

I'm sorry I was snappy today. I was feeling short fused because my stress level was high. I did some meditating to get myself a bit more balanced, and I feel better now.

Omit the word "but." This word does nothing except negate everything you said before it. "I'm sorry but…" No, you're not. You're justifying. Don't justify your behaviours. Instead, own them completely. It's a much more freeing experience, and it leaves him with nothing to retaliate with or feel defensive about.

You never quite understand the power of sorry until you begin incorporating it like this. I can't explain the weight that comes off both of you individually and your relationship as a whole when you bring those two words into your mainstream conversation. It's healing, it's bonding, and it's just plain beautiful.

I have yet to teach this to someone and not hear about its immediate positive effect. Like you, your partner is waiting to be seen and acknowledged. They're waiting to feel like their feelings matter. They're hurt, defensive, and inside they're fearful of the next round of pain.

How would you feel if one day your man came to you and said, "I'm so sorry. For this, and this, and that too. And by the way, I'm not blind to all your efforts. I see you, and I appreciate what you're doing to try and keep us together. I love you for that. Thank you." And then put his arms around you? Wouldn't you soften inside? Wouldn't you open your arms and say, "I love you too?" Wouldn't some of the pain melt away because all that was holding it inside you was the raging anger that it simply wasn't understood?

So do it today. When you see him put your arms around him and say, "I'm sorry I've been so angry and defensive lately. I'm stressed and I let it get the best of me. I know you're doing your best, and I see that. You're a good man, a good father, a good husband. I love you."

And leave it at that. Don't expect anything back from him, and let those words sink in. Then, do it again tomorrow. And the day after. Begin the healing process, and show him how it's accomplished. It's never too late.

CHAPTER 35

Don't Be Afraid to Ask for Comfort

We need comforting. It's another fundamental part of human nature that we seem to forget about in today's culture. Ooo, look at me, I'm so strong and stoic and I don't need anyone cause I've got this all by myself.

Bull.

What's the first thing that happened to us (ideally) when we were born? Our mothers took our little bodies and held us close, comforting us and letting us know that everything was going to be okay. As children people who loved us hugged and kissed our boo-boos away. We let our friends comfort us when we're angry or afraid, so where did we stop feeling like comfort was something that belonged in a relationship?

Hurt and anger become a huge wall between us, and I've seen it time and again where we reject the very thing we most want from our partners, and our relationships become self-fulfilling prophecies of unlovingness. Yes, I made up a word.

"He doesn't love me enough," she cries to her friends, then

rejects his hug and gives him the silent treatment when he comes home. Just like that, anger and hurt keep eroding away at the relationship, taking bite after angry bite until there's nothing left.

I keep saying this, but there's always a choice.

First of all, re-examine your fears. If you're choosing behaviours based on rejection what fears are popping up and directing your actions? Are you rejecting first because you're afraid of putting your true feelings and vulnerabilities out there for fear they'll be rejected? In essence, pre-emptively rejecting him before he can reject you?

Are you afraid of asking to be comforted at all for fear he'll just not cooperate and you'll feel even more hurt than before?

Are you afraid of seeming weak, of losing face, of losing status as top dog by appearing vulnerable?

Are you simply afraid of asking for what you need?

Okay, I get all those. But what about being afraid of losing a good man? What about being afraid of starting over because one day all your pushing away will push him right out of your life? What about being afraid of letting fear drive your actions till you're left standing alone because ultimately you were too afraid to let someone into your most intimate space and love you for everything that you are: the good, the bad, and the ugly?

What if you hide behind all your fears so thoroughly your

partner feels like he has no idea who you really are?

Being vulnerable takes courage. Asking for support takes courage. But we all know that great things are achieved through feats of courage, and it's the same within a relationship. Be brave, step out from behind your fears, and let yourself be completely, honestly human.

A human who comforts and needs comforting. A human who protects and needs protection. A human who gives and receives true and unfiltered love.

Comforting is super simple, and asking should be as simple as the act itself. Here's the thing: Your man wants to make you feel better. He wants you to be happy, and he wants to know he facilitates that. The complicating factor is us women.

Be willing to communicate, and be ready to use as few words as possible. Doing so delivers the message crystal clear, and making it easy for him makes it easy for you to get what you need.

"I need you to put your arms around me and tell me everything is going to be okay" always follows whatever pain I lay out before my husband. Whether it's venting about something crappy that happened today, feeling an overwhelming wave of stress or anxiety, feeling sad, or just wanting to make up after resolving a fight, saying those words to your man are like a gift to him. Suddenly, he knows exactly what to do to make everything okay.

Making it simple to love and comfort you absolutely simplifies love within your relationship. The walls of hurt and anger come down, and with the blockade gone love begins to flow back and forth unrestricted.

This step lays the foundation on which your relationship can be built up and filled with all the love, support, and comfort you need from your partner.

"I've had a really rough day today," you can tell him when he comes home. "I need you to put your arms around me and tell me everything is going to be okay." I've yet to meet a man who doesn't do that on request.

"I had a bad day at work, I need to vent about it. Can you just listen while I do that? Then put your arms around me and tell me everything is going to be okay." Remember that he'll know you're done venting when you say, "Okay, now I need you to put your arms around me and tell me everything is going to be okay."

Did you have a fight? Are you pretty much done getting through it? Wrap it up by saying those magic words, and you'll find both of your feelings come out more soothed and connected.

See, something amazing happens when you allow comforting to replace fear and anger. Oxytocin, that wonder drug your body produces that makes you warm and fuzzy, is released, helping you melt into each other and reconnect with loving feelings. Cortisol is countered, reducing your levels of stress. Dopamine is triggered, telling your brain you feel rewarded.

Oxytocin also has a slight memory fogging effect, which means you'll literally forget some of the depths of pain you felt before getting that hug. Hugging is, in essence, first aid for your feelings. And when it comes to healing, shouldn't your partner be your first line of defense instead of your mortal enemy?

The two of you may be squaring off emotionally right now, standing on opposite sides of enemy lines, but that's not why either of you came into this relationship, and he's as miserable as you are in this standoff. But the moment you introduce this simple trick is the moment you start to come together and really eradicate that invisible line. Now, you're both on the same side.

And isn't that what you really want? To have an ally in this world? Someone who stands by your side as your backup, your army? Because that's what he'll be for you. Your warrior. When something feels tough he's the one waiting to help propel you through it with his love and comfort. It's what you want, and it's what he wants. He just needs you to show him how it's done.

Remember, we are made by design to be each other's healing source. Do you think Mother Nature made a mistake when she made hugs release the chemicals you'd need to feel happy and connected? Nope.

Step 4 – Connect

Every minute of every hour of every day, you hold the power.

CHAPTER 36

Connecting is an Inside Job

"**H**e doesn't get me."

"He doesn't make me happy."

Do you? Understand yourself? Make yourself happy?

That might sound like a couple of smart-alecky questions, but think about it for a second. Have you figured yourself out completely? Do you understand where all your pain and baggage come from, or are you still working through muddled emotions? Have you figured out how to live a life that makes you feel happy, or are you still trying one thing after the next in a quest for some peace of mind and joy in your heart?

I hate to tell you this, but if you're still looking at exterior sources for interior soothing, thinking you'll feel better if the house was cleaner, if you went to the gym more often, if only he'd behave just so, you haven't figured yourself out yet. Because all those things could change, and you'd still be trying to find the magic solution to your inner demons.

True peace happens when you figure out you hold the power to give yourself everything you need.

My mind is racing, so I'm going to give myself some time to meditate.

My body is aching, so I'm going to give myself time to do some yoga.

My heart needs comforting, so I'm going to turn to my man and ask for a hug and some soothing words.

My to-do list feels stressful, so I'm going to give myself permission to delegate some parts and eliminate others.

My self-image is suffering, so I'm going to let the compliments people give me sink in deeper instead of rejecting them.

And the list goes on and on. There are so many ways you can feed yourself what you need. The secret is finding out how to do that and following through. At the end of the day it's not fair to ask your partner to do something you're not willing to do yourself, and unless you learn how to make yourself happy how can you possibly ask him to make you happy? It's pretty much a cart before the horse scenario.

So tap into yourself. Moment by moment, day by day. Make yourself a priority. Take moments of stillness so you can hear the voice inside your head. Not the nagging, negative ego voice. The other one, the one that's vulnerable and truthful and full of love. You'll know the difference when you pay attention to what direction it tells you to take – if it says someone else needs to do something to make you happy, that's your ego voice. When it gives you a directive that involves your actions and yours alone, that's the one to listen to.

If you're worried people will call you selfish for taking more time to take care of yourself, stop being concerned about the opinions of others at the expense of your own well-being. Nobody but you knows just how to feed your soul, and their ego and fears of coming second or third shouldn't come between you and your inner peace.

Am I saying to never again be of service to your loved ones? No! But spreading all your capacity for love outward without dispensing any on yourself puts you in danger of running out of energy and having nothing left to give. Fill your tank, and you'll have so much more to distribute. And not just more, but the quality will be uh-may-zing.

Think about the example you'll set within your family. Your beaming face, positive energy, and genuine love and care will be hard to miss, and they'll start to wonder how they themselves can take part in something that looks so great. How can showing those around you what true happiness looks like be selfish? You're always a teaching tool, remember that. Are you going to set an example on how to be unhappy? Or are you going to radiate happiness?

Start to really dream about what you want from life, and create a vision board. Let your intuition guide you when flipping through magazines and tear out anything and everything that appeals to you. No dream is too big. One of my favourite sayings is "Reach for the stars and at the very least you'll hit the top of the trees."

Meditate, meditate, meditate. This clears the noise in your head and really puts you in tune with what your soul desires. There's a lot of shouting going on all around you. Your ego, your conditioning, your history, and people who want to pull you in different directions can become really loud inside our minds. Meditation lets your inner voice break through and helps you answer the question you need to ask yourself the most. What do I want?

If something pops up but you hesitate, ask yourself this: "What am I afraid of? Judgement? Rejection? Making others unhappy? What are the consequences of responding to my fears instead of my desires?" Write them down. Clarify them by making them visible. Boogeymen have a hard time surviving when the light is turned on.

Let me give you an example. Say you've had a dream for years about becoming a pastry chef. You have two little ones, and time and money are short, and you keep pushing your dream aside. What are you afraid of? Taking time away from your family and being resented? Being more tired because you've added to your already busy schedule?

What are the consequences of responding to your fears instead of your desires? Feeling unhappy that you're living more for others than for yourself? Feeling unfulfilled? Feeling like you're sleepwalking through life? Dying before you've even tried to make a dream come true?

Maybe you should fear never teaching your children that they can accomplish anything they set their minds to because it's not something you modeled. Maybe you should fear never letting your family see how passion can light up your eyes and make you excited. Or not letting those who love you show you how supportive they can be.

In the order of things, when you're working on making your relationship better it should be 1) I figure myself out, 2) I teach people what I need, and 3) I make others happy.

Start at the beginning. Stop trying to force goodness from the outside in, and start creating it from the inside out. Your happiness contribution to your relationship is equal to the happiness you've created within yourself. Are you feeling lost, unhappy, confused? Or are you feeling whole, satisfied, and clear about what you're working towards?

We are all a work in progress, at all times, but this moment is as important as the next. What do you want? I give you permission to answer that question and begin your quest. Those who love you will love you more because the happiness you create will not only light up your eyes, it'll light up their hearts, and in the end they too will strive for more goodness within themselves.

CHAPTER 37

Celebrate

I learned somewhere along the line that the best way to greet someone was by exhibiting a mini celebration at their presence. There's something about walking into a room and feeling like you just lit it up that makes you feel amazing, and it's a gift I consciously began to share with people.

"Hiiiiiii!!!" *You're here and that's goooooood!!!* I'd express when my husband came home, when friends came over, when my girlfriend's kids walked into the room. I started to celebrate people and saw them light up at feeling welcomed with wide open arms and an even wider smile.

I rejoiced at their presence and honored their place in my life. I praised the goodness in them. Every time I saw them was cause for a mini moment of joy, and together we feasted on the minute of happiness that it created.

There's something about happiness that builds on itself in a compound interest sort of way. The more you do it, the more it grows. Bigger and faster and more abundant, that emotion becomes a habit instead of something you have to dig deep to find. And let's not forget that focusing on the moments that make you happy releases some pretty awesome chemicals in you like dopamine, while the hug you exchange releases oxytocin, both of which have long lasting, positive effects on your brain.

I learned to be generous with kindness and positive feelings, breathing extra life into them and sharing that energy wherever I went. My husband started coming through the door with a smile on his face. People started lighting up when I walked into a room, telling me the vibe changed the moment I got there.

My inner celebration became like a force field against negativity, and I found that other people's poopy moods just rolled off me like water off a duck. I'd shrug my shoulders, saying "meh" whenever someone complained about another person's bad attitudes. "Whatever," I'd say. "Let them do them, and you do you."

I found myself having mini moments of celebration all by myself, usually when I was driving. I'd let myself ride those moments, surrendering to them like I'd learned to surrender to my negative feelings. Breathing into them, I'd let myself become fully immersed in the happy sensations, digging deep for every last bit and letting them fill my body.

And something switched.

I began to have happy cries.

Great big, sobbing, heaving, happy cries filled with joy and gratitude. It was…. Wonderful. Magical. Beautiful.

I'd gone from wanting to no longer exist to feeling peaceful about my existence, and from there to feeling grateful to have this life full of beauty and love and possibility.

Inside out, I began to re-create the world I lived in and what I worked on bringing forth changed the emotional tone of my life, causing happiness and instilling joy.

Listen, feelings are going to happen. The good, the bad, the ugly. All of them will cycle through you at all phases of your life. Meditation and learning how to blow up my negative feelings didn't mean I'd never experience them again, it meant I learned to release them instead of pushing them down and accumulating them to unmanageable levels.

I had to learn how to deal with my negative feelings and focus on ways to sink into my positive ones, but it's these release and immersion techniques that makes me so happy today. Understand that brain is an incredible tool, and while we're far from understanding it completely, what we do know today gives you the power to improve your life. Failing to acknowledge that and implement these simple strategies until they become second nature is like failing to drink a glass of water when you're dying of thirst.

CHAPTER 38

Ride the Waves

By temporarily disconnecting from my husband I was able to re-connect with him on a whole new level. Let me explain what happened and how it saved us.

I use the term "spinning" a lot because it captures what seemed to be happening inside me on a constant basis. Round and round my thoughts and emotions would spin, circling around my man and what he could be thinking and feeling.

I hated the thought that we had discord, but I had a lot of anger too, so I'd whirl back and forth between trying to figure out how I could fix what was wrong and reacting fiercely to what was pissing me off.

I love him, I want to amend this.

I hate him, he's such an asshole.

It was a ride that was driving me crazy, and I finally had to push myself off before I spun myself into pure insanity. And let me tell you, it got pretty close to that.

I keep saying what's inside you is infecting those around you, and I mean it. In this state of mind there was nothing I could do that would fix our relationship. The desperation, the craziness, the discomfort, the inability to see and feel clearly all kept me miles from a solution that would actually help us. It was a forest for the trees scenario – there was no way I'd be able to clearly see how I could help us heal if I wasn't helping myself first.

So I took a step back. I extracted my thoughts and emotions from his. He's angry? So be it. I'll let him deal with himself for now while I focus on dealing with me. He's stressed, emotional, frustrated, and unhappy? Not my problem today; I'm facing my own feelings instead of trying to mend his.

I untangled myself from him, bit by bit. Internally shrugging my shoulders became a new habit, and I'd shrug off his bad moods every time he walked through the door with them. Not my chair, not my problem.

Like me he was trying to make his way through his own quagmire of pent up feelings, of shitty history, of pain that started piling up long before we ever got together, and the blind leading the blind through unfamiliar territory never worked. There wasn't anything I could do for him until I'd learned what I could do for myself, and so I separated myself from his thoughts and feelings and stopped myself from even thinking about them when they popped up in my head.

"No!" my inner coach would say when my mind started to stray towards him and how I could fix our relationship. *Focus on yourself.*

I started to ride his emotions, staying on top of them instead of getting pulled underneath. I stopped rolling round and round, getting pushed and pulled and sucked under his emotional waves while desperately trying to swim back up, and I stopped gagging and swallowing and flailing in his waters.

I couldn't save him. Not in the state I was in. Not while I was drowning myself.

So I pushed back from him. I took the chance that while I was learning to swim he might drown, but it was either save myself and maybe save us or watch us both go down.

Meditation gave me the tools I needed to see myself through that process because shrinking my amygdala made me capable of being less reactive to his moods. I stopped internalizing his feelings and let him take responsibility for them, just like I was taking responsibility for mine.

Surfing became my new emotional talent. I became an expert at riding just about anybody's feelings. I'm not saying I've never been affected since I taught myself to surf, but every time I get knocked off my board I shake it off, incorporate some understanding for that particular wave, and get right back on.

I started thinking about a passage from the Bible, about when Jesus was crucified on the cross and he said "Father, forgive them, for they know not what they are doing" (don't ask me how I remember that from my few years of going to church as a child). I compared it to how people will be affected by their overactive amygdala and in turn vomit their negative emotions on those around them, trying to pin an exterior source for their interior pain like I'd been doing.

I stepped back and stopped feeling hurt by his emotions and actions. I stopped focusing on what he was or wasn't doing. I stopped revolving my emotional world around him.

Not.

My.

Problem.

And because I wasn't taking on his feelings anymore and was dealing solely with mine I started to really get through all my own pain, to figure out how to make myself happy, and to become a center of peacefulness and contentment.

And my husband had no choice but to face his own feelings head on, because I was no longer blocking his view of them with mine.

See, lumping my feelings with his made them indistinguishable in his head, and he was able to blame me for his suffering. Once I stepped back, took mine in hand, and stopped blaming him he was left to face that he owned his experiences, and he took another emotional dive. "Maybe I'm just fucked up," he said one day as he cradled his head in his hands. I'd seen that same broken look in the mirror not too long ago.

"It's going to be okay, baby," I was able to say as I put my arms around him. I knew it hurt to face himself, but I also knew it could be done victoriously. And so it was in this way that I took my turn to become the pillar of strength in our relationship, letting him process and work through his emotions as they washed over him.

It's because I'd learned how to swim that I wasn't pulled under while he struggled. And it was because I had developed the strength to stay afloat that I could extend the love and compassion he needed during his own darkest hours.

All that being said, I have a message for you. It's been bouncing at me in various forms the last few days, and now I realize why as I write this chapter.

Ladies, pain is your friend. Pain is what shows you what's wrong. Pain isn't meant to be avoided, it's meant to be used as a signal that change is necessary. When we dull pain with pain killers, drugs, alcohol, or whatever else in an effort to avoid feeling we unconsciously hurt ourselves, and eventually that all catches up and now we're crippled because we didn't do what we should have to deal with the problem. Avoidance is never a real solution. It's simply a short term Band-Aid that eventually bites us in the ass.

Make friends with pain. Make it your ally. Something you can tolerate and actually appreciate because you start to see it as a functional wake up call. It's a push towards growth, a self-improvement tool, and it'll make your life better if you can lean into it.

Do you know what the opposite of pain is? The absence of pain. And when you realize after suffering that you have an absence of pain and you've earned it by working through whatever was wrong, that your relief and joy are real and true and genuine, that's where the real magic happens. That's when you know you've achieved something freaking unbelievable, and that's when you start to have happy cries.

Become a master at handling pain and you'll become a master at handling happiness. I promise.

CHAPTER 39

The Words Coming Out of Your Mouth

I sat with a group of ladies the other night and noticed something. Often in relationships we're asking for the opposite behaviour of what we're actually conveying and wondering why we're not getting what we want. "Do what I say, not what I do!" my mom used to say to me when I was growing up, and even as a child I knew that was unfair.

It's natural for us to mimic the behaviour of those around us. In a developmental context it's how we learn, both consciously and subconsciously. Monkey see, monkey do, right?

So as kids we learned how to clean a house or hunt deer because our parents showed us, but we also learned how to communicate with people by watching what our parents did or said. If we had racially biased parent's chances are we picked up the same mentality, and if we had hard working parents we likely strived to work just as hard to achieve what we wanted.

In a social context we often imitate our peer groups out of a subconscious fear of rejection, and even if that behaviour is dysfunctional there's still a drive in us to conform. "Pack mentality" is a term used to describe why people who otherwise wouldn't dream of taking part in a riot will join a group lighting fires and pushing over cars.

Imitation is ingrained in our DNA, so it's no surprise that your partner will likely respond in kind to whatever you put out there.

"I want him to stop talking to me like I'm one of the kids!" said someone at a party I was at. "I even took him aside the other night and let him know he needs to stop talking to me like a child." We all nodded in agreement. It certainly seemed like a fair enough request.

This conversation took place at a house party when the men were in the garage drinking beer while us ladies sipped our cocktails in the living room, and not long after her husband walked through on his way to the sliding back door.

"What are you doing?" she asked him as he whisked by.

"Grabbing more beer," he replied as he headed to the patio.

"Outside in the dark with no shoes on?" Without a word or glance he continued on his way out and reappeared with a new case of beer, disappearing once again in the garage.

Her pet peeve was being talked to like a child who didn't know better, yet here she was confronting him like a seven year old who needed to be scolded for making bad decisions. Do you think at some point he might complain to his friends that his wife talks to him like he's one of the kids?

Which one of them started exhibiting a parental role instead of husband or wife role? It doesn't matter. What matters is breaking the pattern and leading a new way of being together.

Listen to what you're complaining about. Start writing it down if you need to clarify the things that really bother you in your relationship. Then start paying attention to the words leaving your lips. Are you doing the same things you're bugged by? Know that it's not fair to ask for anything you're not doing first, so until you become an agent of change yourself it's not fair to ask him to be any different.

If you can point to the last few months and say, "Baby, when was the last time you feel I talked to you like you're one of the kids? I know I used to do that, and I'm sorry, I was stressed and I wasn't paying attention to how I was reacting. But I've stopped now. How long has it been since I've done that? (Give him time to think at this point) I know I've been trying to not do it for a few months now. I'd like it if you stopped too. I think we can communicate better, don't you? I'm going to keep trying. I'm not telling you what to do, but I feel I need to be in a relationship where we stop micro managing each other and talk to each other as partners instead of parenting each other. I love you, and I'm trying every day to be a better partner. I hope you can see that and will try with me."

Remember, time and consistency are your ally here. Time for him to realize that what you're saying is true. Time to change his own habit and adjust. Time for both him and you to have slip ups and recover without punishment. Time to really change while you consistently apply this new way of being.

I know you've heard this quote by Ghandi: "We but mirror the world," he said. "All the tendencies present in the outer world are to be found in the world of our body. If we could change ourselves, the tendencies in the world would also change. As a man changes his own nature, so does the attitude of the world change towards him. This is the divine mystery supreme. A wonderful thing it is and the source of our happiness. We need not wait to see what others do."

You have the power to create the relationship you want. I know this because I changed everything in mine, and I know this because I've taught so many women to change everything in theirs. I have email after email from women who've modified a few simple things in their behaviours and absolutely transformed their partners, and now thank me for the depth of happiness they're experiencing today.

I didn't tell them how to get their men to change. I told them how to change what they said and what they did, and the results were swift. You want a more supportive man? Be more supportive. You want a more adult relationship? Treat him like an adult. Whatever you want, be and do.

I know it sounds over simplistic, but keep in mind the theory of Occam's Razor: The simplest solution tends to be the best one.

Be able to point to yourself when you have conversations

about change in your relationship. "I've been meditating and it's calming me. I'm not feeling as reactive anymore. I'm not feeling as stressed anymore. I don't want to fight anymore. I'm changing myself, and I've been changing my behaviours. It's been a few months since I've (insert change here). (Let him think about this for a second, while he goes through his memory data bank to confirm what you're saying.) And I'm going to keep changing and working at all this. You know, the best predictor of future behaviour is past behaviour and I'm creating a new history, with new ways of being. I'm feeling happier today, and I'm feeling optimistic about the future. I'd love for you to meet me where I am."

Do this lovingly. Patiently. Show him and let him absorb the truth of this new reality. Give him an opportunity to reconnect with the new you. All this doesn't happen in one day. In fact, it took almost a full year from when I started to meditate before I noticed my husband really settle into our new way and shed his anxiety that we'd revert to our old methods and start to fight again.

But that was okay. I kept working on myself, and the meditation I was doing gave me patience and kept me from feeling anxious about the transition time. And don't forget what happens when we dance together – taking one step back creates a space for our partner to take one step forward.

CHAPTER 40

Safe Space for Dialogue

I know how frustrating it can be when you want your partner to hear what you have to say, only to have him push your words aside and bulldoze over them with his own complaints.

I know what it's like to sit on an issue for days, maybe even weeks, waiting for the right moment to bring them up because you're trying so hard to not rock the boat or complain non-stop. To finally ask him to sit down and have a conversation with you about what's on your mind only to feel like nothing has been resolved because he took over the time you'd set aside to put all his pent up baggage on the table.

I know what it's like to feel like your feelings don't seem to matter. To feel like you're never getting anywhere. To feel like you can never figure out how to come to a resolution about something once and for all.

Sister, I hear you, and this is how I finally found a way around all that.

Consider this – what if he's feeling the exact same way? See, men are pretty good at hiding their feelings and thoughts. Too good, actually, and we forget that they actually have them. But what they're doing is telling themselves, "I'm just going to put my head down and power through the next (week, months, years) doing my job as a man and doing my best to avoid conflict."

They've got all kinds of issues going through their minds, but they push them aside until the day we decide to open the floodgates, and like a sneaky opportunist they take their chance.

She wants to open up that can of worms? Okay, while we're at it, here's mine.

And in his rush to get all his stuff out he forgets we had anything to say in the first place, and all that's going through his mind is, "Where's my resolution?"

It seems selfish, right? But why is his desires for settlement any different from yours? You're both wanting to air your grievances, but the fact is when two people want to talk at the same time nobody gets heard.

In an ideal world when you choose a time to go first he would sit and listen patiently, let you know that you're heard and understood, and then air his own grievances and allow you to let him know that he's heard and understood too. But I think we can all agree that we don't live in an ideal world, and some mental re-arranging has to take place to accommodate reality.

Let's face the fact that historically, trying to go first doesn't usually work because even if words aren't leaving his lips the mental chatter in his head is keeping him from fully hearing you. Every issue you're bringing up is being met with a mental "yeah but" so loud that nothing you say is being validated. Frustrating, right?

It's crappy cause it's true, and something's gotta change.

You want him to be able to understand your pain, to connect with your heart, and to be the sort of man who'll have the desire to help you make things better. You want him to hear out your problems and to take part in finding solutions together. Yes?

So guess what. You've gotta go first and show him just how that's done.

Put aside every argument that's popping up in your head right now, telling you to do anything but that. Look at your history and ask yourself, "Has anything else worked?" If the answer is no, then what have you got to lose?

Are you afraid of losing face? Of giving up the upper hand? How much of either do you have when your relationship is swirling round in a dysfunctional toilet bowl, about to be flushed down?

What are you listening to when the idea of letting him unload everything that's on his mind first causes a hot flash of frustration? Your ego? How far has your ego gotten you when it comes to real, lasting intimate love?

I know you want to be heard, so let me teach you how to listen.

First, set yourself up mentally to assume that the next time you sit down to hash things out he's going to go first. I mean, really prepare for that so when it happens you're not feeling pushed aside. Trust me, your time will come once you follow these steps.

Now that you're already prepared to let him go first, schedule some talk time. "Babe, I've got some stuff I want to talk to you about. When would be a good time?" Letting him choose the time gives him a way to feel better in tune with having a deep conversation. Men are compartmentalizers; they need to put away what's happening in their heads right now in order to prepare for what's going to happen next. If he says, "I don't know," then ask him to let you know when would be a good time within a reasonable timeframe. "Okay, can you let me know by Wednesday when would be a good time? I just need about ten minutes."

This lets him know you're not trying to push his boundaries and you're respecting where his brain is at right now, but still want some level of cooperation. Remind him on Wednesday if he doesn't get back to you before then. Keep in mind that he doesn't fully realize that you're practicing a new you, and he might be wary that this conversation is going to start a fight. Patience. Meditate. Maintain and build your Zen and keep separating your peace of mind from his actions.

When you finally sit down to talk, start bringing your stuff forward, using "I feel" statements. Anything that starts with "you" feels attacky (yes, I made up another word). "I feel like I need more help," "I feel tired, overwhelmed, sad."

This keeps him from feeling like you're pointing a finger and accusing him, which keeps him from shutting down in defense. In the beginning he might become defensive as a knee jerk reaction, but ignore it and remind him that you're just talking about your feelings and aren't blaming anything on him. Remember, defensive people don't hear a thing, and you want to teach him how to hear you.

Now, because you opened up the gates it's possible he's going to pour all his stuff out. Good. You want him to because once it's all done he'll finally be able to hear you. Let him bring out the first issue. You don't do this, you haven't been doing that, you promised this but didn't deliver. Don't be defensive, don't counter attack, don't minimize, and don't let your ego pop up and deny what he's saying. Those are his feelings and thoughts, and like yours, he has every right to them. He may be wrong, but so what? He needs validation just like you would.

Show him how it's done.

Hear out that first issue. Then let him know you fully understood it, repeat it back to him till he agrees you get it, and find a solution together. Write it down to go on the fridge. Then, ask him what else is on his mind because he won't hear you until his brain is completely cleared of all the backed up junk that's accumulated.

You: "Babe, I'm feeling like I have too much to do at home with the two babies and the cleaning and working. I feel really stressed and overwhelmed."

Him: "Well, when I come home I'm tired too! And all you do is complain about what I'm not doing, and you don't notice what I'm actually doing around here."

You: "You're saying that you feel unappreciated for what you're doing when you're home?"

Him: "Yes. And I did this and I did that, and it's really annoying when I come home and you're forcing a to-do list down my throat and saying the kids are driving you crazy all the time."

You: "Okay, help me understand how you're feeling. That you feel like I just want you to do stuff all the time and I don't let you have any peace at home?"

Him: "Yeah. I'd like to be able to come home and just have a few minutes of peace."

You: "So what you're saying is it's stressful for you when you come home."

Him: "Yes."

You: "Okay, I get that you feel stressed when you come home because I hit you with stuff right away. I'm sorry for that. I let things build up and I explode on you. That's not fair to you. What can I do to make that better?"

Him: "Well, you can give me some time to settle in before you come at me with requests."

You: "Okay, I understand you need some time to switch gears from work mode to home/husband/daddy mode when you get here. How much time would work for you?"

Him: "An hour would be nice."

You: "Okay, babe, I can do that. I'll wait an hour to let you settle into being home before asking for anything. I love you. What else?"

Now, I want you to read that exchange again and switch the roles. Don't you want him to be able to do this for you? To sit patiently through your angst, show you he listened and understood and looked to find a solution with you, and then wanted to know what else was weighing you down? Yeah, you do. That's why you have to show him how it's done.

What else are the two magical words that'll finally get you heard. What else tells him you're open to everything that's on his mind, and what else will drain everything that's buzzing between his ears. What else will finally get you everything you want from him.

Because when you've what elsed the crap out of him and there's nothing left he's going to look at you and say, "What about you? What's bothering you?"

When the walls of defensiveness and unresolved issues are taken down it's your open communication that will finally help connect you. Put ego aside, apologize for his hurt feelings, show him you're open to solutions, let him empty his mind and heart, and let him bridge the distance with his own willingness to do the same for you.

Connect with him, his mind, his heart, his feelings, his sensitivity, and he'll connect with yours. When it comes to a real, lasting intimate relationship generosity needs a place at the table. Be gracious, be magnanimous, be generous, and he'll follow suit because he'll finally learn what that looks like in a relationship.

CHAPTER 41

Be Predictable

D o you know the scariest thing that crosses a man's mind when he's driving home from work? "What's she going to be like today?"

Yep, Ladies, we are the untamed lion in our men's lives. And that uncertainty of whether we're going to bite and slash on sight creates a certain amount of fear and anxiety in him even before he steps through the door, making him that much harder to deal with if we need extra support because his pre-emptive stress puts him on edge.

Predictability is a human necessity, because the opposite signals nothing but potential danger in our minds. Let's take another walk into the past, shall we?

There we are, cavemen and cavewomen trying to survive in a world where danger is high and our defenses are low. We need to be able to predict what will happen when we do certain things and go certain places because what we don't foresee has dangerous consequences. This is where the term "fear of the unknown" originates from, the notion that what we don't know could kill us.

But when you're constantly alert and cautious, where in your emotional behaviour is there room for love, patience, and care? If I'm always on guard for what might hurt me how do I cultivate the mind space to be looking out for how to make my partner happy? We can only give what we currently have within us, so when you think about the peace you want from your partner on a regular basis you realize that you need to help him achieve that particular state of mind first.

Becoming predictable in your behaviours helps him gain that peace of mind, and his inner peace will become a source of loving, supportive patience down the road. If he can predict that each and every time he comes home you're going to give him a hug and a kiss no matter how stressed you got that day, he's going to come prepared to be your white knight because he's been looking forward to seeing you, his beautiful and loving partner, instead of fearing the lion at the gate.

Now hear me out. Predictability doesn't mean you won't rampage from time to time because today was super overwhelming and you're hormonal on top of that, but if he can also predict you'll take responsibility for your momentary blow ups and apologize for them with a hug and a kiss and the words "I'm sorry, babe, that wasn't about you, it was about my stressful day and my hormones," his brain will stay relaxed.

My husband can predict that no matter what, I'm going to make his coffee and toast in the morning. He can predict that I'll usually be in a good mood. And he can predict that when I get grumpy because my hormone replacement therapy is kicking into high gear I'm going to come to him later and say I'm sorry. There's nothing scary about me or our relationship because I've made things easy to navigate and understand, and I never feel that we're disconnected because when we have our mood swings we can both predict that it's going to be A-Okay when all is said and done.

Forgiveness has become a predictable factor between us. Understanding, love, patience, kisses, gratitude, appreciation, are all as predictable as occasionally taking responsibility and s'plaining those moments when we implode. Relationships are roller coasters, but you can smooth out the ride and turn it into a railroad simply by making even your off moments predictably forgiveable.

Relationships function best when minds are at ease. You're working at smoothing yours out through meditation, and you can influence his state of mind by creating a deep sense of stability within your relationship. Connection, the kind that feels like you're attached far deeper than the eye can see, happens when it feels safe to be intricately woven with you without fear of sudden pain.

I asked my husband today, "How happy does it make you knowing I'm going to be the same every time you come home?" He said, "I wouldn't use the word happy, I'd say comforting."

Comforted. Don't you want to feel comforted by your man? Help him achieve that feeling so he can spread it all over you in return. Be predictable. Make it your mission to smile and give him a hug and a kiss every time he comes through the door. You'll both love what that creates.

Step 5 – Discovery

It's never too late to redefine everything.

CHAPTER 42

The Joy of Giving

Now that you're consciously tearing down the walls of ego, hurt, and anger that kept you disconnected it's time to really plug back into each other and rediscover the joy that brought you together in the first place.

Long before your baggage came out and created discord, long before life got hectic and created anger, there was something special. A spark, a chemistry, and a longing to be each other's greatest source of love.

Do you remember that time? When all you thought about was how happy he made you, and when the next thought was "What can I do in return?" When you couldn't wait to be together again so you could talk and cuddle and kiss till life's requirements forced you to re-enter what you called "the real world." That's right, there was a time when your relationship seemed so amazing it was unreal.

Well, guess what? You can get back to that feeling, plus plus. That honeymoon phase can become reality all over again, with an added bonus that this time: It's truly real.

This time, instead of being fed by the beautiful chemicals our brains release in an effort to drive us to procreation we can experience a lifelong honeymoon period borne of deep, mutual love and respect for each other. And the emotional sensation is out of this world.

Imagine this.

You're driving home from work. It's been a stressful day, but nothing you weren't able to handle and work through, and you release a few lingering shreds of anxiety in your car as you make your way home. You know there's no point worrying tonight about something you'll be resolving tomorrow, and you whisper the word "surrender" a few times under your breath, allowing it to replace the buzzing in your mind with the comforting knowledge that you've got everything in hand.

You take a moment to be grateful for the peace of mind you're able to achieve thanks to your regular commitment to meditation, and you feel like you're forgetting the constant hum of anxiety you used to experience. It's been a while since you stopped being shocked at the effects your shrunken amygdala is having on your general well-being, but you're still conscious of how drastic the change has been and you're loving it. You're aware that you're smiling more and you kind of feel like Tinker Bell, sprinkling pixie dust all over the place with your positivity and unflappable attitude.

You pull up the driveway and see your man's car, and a smile crosses your face. Gone are the days when you'd be nervously driving home, wondering what would happen when you got there. Who would be the first to start the fight? Who would have the shortest fuse? How would he react to your request that he help with a chore? How would you react to his silence? Those days seem faded now, a thing of the distant past, because you've created a new way of being together and it seems to be taking hold.

You feel… happy.

You walk in the door and call out a cheerful "Hi, babe!"

"Hi, baby!" he replies, and following the sound of his voice you find him in the kitchen putting away the groceries he picked up on the way home. He stops and walks towards you, putting his arms around your waist as he leans in for a kiss. "I love you!" you can't help exclaiming, cupping his face in your hands and kissing him tenderly.

"How was your day?" he asks as he resumes putting food in the cupboard.

"Meh," you reply. "I knew the afternoon meeting would go long. It was kind of frustrating because a lot of the stuff we talked about has already been figured out. It felt like I was trying to explain fractions to a four year old."

"That sucks," he says. It's a simple statement, and you're happy to end it there and move on, happy that you can have a simple conversation about work stress without it turning into a big discussion about what you should and shouldn't be doing or feeling. He's become great at just listening, and you feel another surge of love for him.

You walk over and wrap your arms around his waist. "I'm making that lasagna dish you really like tonight."

"Oh yeah?" His eyes light up, and he hugs you tight. "My baby's so good to me!" You lift your face and he plants another, longer kiss on your lips.

With a full, happy heart you set about making supper while he heads outside and gets some yard work done. You eat side by side on the couch watching TV and occasionally one of you reaches out to stroke a leg, and after dinner you take a moment to cuddle with him on the couch before heading into your office to get some work done. Or you and he take on mom and dad duties and get the kids ready for bed. Regardless of whether or not it's a parental life, you're stealing little moments of sweetness. Touches and kindness and happy glances reign, each moment building on the last.

You get to bed and cuddle close together. Your emotional closeness feels so big that even feeling him glued to you as he assumes the big spoon position seems too far away. You reach back and put your hand on his thigh, drawing him closer as you scooch into him.

"I love you, baby," you say, and he kisses your neck affectionately. "Thank you for being so amazing."

"Thank *you* for being so amazing!" he replies, and the happiness in his voice makes you feel like your heart is going to bust out of your chest. *I can't believe how awesome this is*, you think as you begin to sink into sleep.

This whole scenario is not a dream. It's not an unreal, impossible world, and it's not something that's beyond your reach. This is what happens when you strip away what stands between your humanity and his, and let yourself practice habits borne of love instead of pain within your relationships.

Allowance, understanding, harmony, love. It's all there for the taking, but only when you yourself decide to incorporate it above all else.

Have you ever heard the saying, It's the little things that count? Remember when you used to thrive on all the little things you did for each other? When each little act of kindness seemed big enough to keep your love floating on a cloud?

What happened?

Did they get replaced by the day to day tasks of dealing with real life? Did they get pushed aside by stress, anger, and withheld by feelings of revenge for the slights you suffered when he stopped doing them himself?

Did all those little things get replaced by work and mommyhood and a feeling that being perfunctory with each other was the new adulting? Did you forget how good it felt to be kind?

Your relationship went through evolution after evolution, and it's not done yet. What's the next phase going to be? Let me answer that for you. Kindness.

Kindness. Sounds kind of vague, doesn't it? Like the word 'nice.' So let me clear that up with more word association.

Affection. Thoughtfulness. Sympathy. Benevolence. Gentleness. Good will. Forgiveness.

A relationship punctuated with little things throughout the day, growing and growing until being of service to each other becomes second nature. You need to rediscover the joy of helping each other because it's this reconnection with loving actions that gives you the strength to finally get through the bigger issues.

We used to be in tune with that part of our humanity. Our cavemen relied on us to keep the fires burning while they went hunting, and they appreciated the warmth when they got back. We relied on them to bring us protein rich foods and prepared it while they taught the young ones to make sharp knives and become proficient hunters like themselves. We were constantly, harmoniously, and lovingly being of service to each other because it was how we survived generation after generation.

I know life feels harder now. Raising kids was done as a group, giving us breaks while someone else took over for a moment. Work, when done by many, seemed less overwhelming and became part of our vital socializing. Our brains had more opportunities to rest as we devoted ourselves to repetitive tasks in nature.

This new way of being, living in nuclear families in separate homes, doing things all by ourselves and being expected to like it, raising kids and having our mistakes magnified because we didn't have an older, more experienced adult to take over when we were fatigued can wear away at our relationships like wood rubbing on rope, fraying it till it snaps.

I'm not saying your frustrations aren't valid. I'm not saying you're wrong to feel how you feel. What I'm saying is if you want something different you're the one who can get the ball rolling, and rolling right.

You're the one who's going to do a 180 and do something different today, and tomorrow, and the day after. You're the one who's going to put on a different face and start infusing your relationship with what you want till it overflows, making both your cups run over.

You're the one who's going to re-discover the joy of service to your partner, and you're the one who's going to say "Thank you!" when he reciprocates.

You're going to stop keeping score and saying "I'll do this when he does that." You're going to pick up his favourite chocolate bar at the store. Put away up his clothes without a word. Give him a kiss on the cheek and take his hand when you're walking, all because you're behaving today in the way you want your relationship to look tomorrow.

And if you do all this and it doesn't work? Then you've practiced being amazing and you've earned your way out. And when you meet a man who'll appreciate this new attitude because it's how he's always wanted to be in a relationship you'll have exactly what you've been striving for.

If you are *this* woman and he's selfish, demeaning, and lazy, then you're with a guy and not a man, and you need to get out. Because when you're *this* woman a real man makes you feel like *gold*. Period.

Nothing you do is uncompensated, and that goes for either end of the behaviour spectrum. If you're cold and withholding, then that's exactly the sort of relationship you're setting yourself up for. If you become kind and serviceable then it doesn't matter how long you've been together, eventually it turns the tide – unless you're with a total douchebag. In which case you'll need to take all your goodness and spread it where it'll be received with grace, appreciation, and love.

Listen, there is a lot left to uncover when it comes to your relationship with this person. You're set to discover just how happy you can be. You'll discover how deep your pain resides, and how deeply you can love and feel joy. You'll get to see how sensitive your partner is and appreciate how you can impact how much they smile and laugh.

You might discover a whole new you as weight lifts off your shoulders and you really start to look inside and draw out the long lost dreams you stuffed down. Your emotions will feel different. Your days will change, and you'll discover an existence you never imagined.

You have an entire new world to discover. I don't say this lightly: There's so much more than you know right now.

Step 6 – Intimacy

It's okay to be human. It's when we don't know how to be a human being that we fight with those we love.

CHAPTER 43

This Is Your Brain on Issues

What wouldn't you give to be able to open your head and put your brain on the table so you could walk away from it once in a while? Men look at us like we're some kind of crazy sometimes because they can't understand how our minds can drive us a little, or a lot, out of whack.

They operate on a different system than ours, utilizing a "one file at a time" mental approach to thinking instead of the "everything and the kitchen sink" way we load up our minds. They don't understand the layered chatter that can fill our thoughts, and how all the ideas can sometimes feel like a stadium full of people talking at the same time.

See men like to weigh one thing at a time, while we tend to multitask. But sometimes our multitasking goes overboard and we can't understand anything over the din inside our heads, and instead of sitting down and trying to sort out the voices one by one and analyzing which ones make sense we begin to react blindly in an attempt to justify our confused feelings.

I had my own run-in with this recently and found myself at an emotional crossroads. Here's what I did to get me through the moment:

Last night my husband was watching football while I worked away in my office, making sure *Comeback Queen* would be ready for my editor to dive into the next morning. Having finally reached my 'good enough' moment I went to the living room and started asking questions about why he didn't want the Raiders to win the game playing on TV. Instead of answering my third question he stayed silent, and I got offended at being ignored. After a brief scuffle I took my injured ego and went off to bed, alone.

As I lay there I began coming up with reasons to justify my bruised feelings. He was a jerk for ignoring me. He'd been acting a bit off for the past weeks, this was just the tip of the iceberg, and what I didn't know about the negativity in his mind would to lead to our demise. He didn't respect me enough. We were going to become more and more distant until this marriage ended in divorce too. What was I going to do when our relationship ended?

On and on my brain went unchecked for about five minutes, till I realized I was layering one thought over the next while doing nothing to clear any of them. But the worst part was each thought came accompanied with its own emotion. Not only was my head filled with a multitude of different opinions on what had just happened, but my body was filled with a bunch of negative feelings too, all mixing and jumbling until I couldn't tell one from the other.

Stop it, I told myself.

Stop letting my imagination run away from me. Stop letting my thoughts continue unchecked, and stop letting another idea come forth until I'd done my due diligence and formulated whether or not the previous one had any place inside my head and heart.

Stop it.

I lay there and focused on clearing my mind instead of giving in to the turmoil inside my head. I relaxed my body, conscious of how tense my muscles had become while my thoughts ran unchecked. I asked myself, *How am I feeling?* Then I named the emotions that were swirling within me. Hello, fear. Hello, anxiety. I didn't attempt to associate them to any particular thoughts, instead turning my attention to just letting them be, letting them grow, and letting them run their course and deplete themselves once they'd run out of steam.

I didn't need to be angry. I didn't need to feel insecure. I didn't need to start planning couples therapy so I could prevent our relationship from becoming another doomed statistic. I needed to stop thinking, I needed to release the emotions that had happened while my brain had sprinted off on me, and I needed to relax.

So I did, and eventually I drifted off to sleep, my little Lulu cuddling beside me in my hubby's spot as I let him fall asleep in front of the TV.

The next morning I woke up, the partially closed bedroom door letting me know he'd dressed in the room across the hall, being quiet to not wake me. "Lulu, do you want to take the elevator?" I asked her, as she stood on the edge of the bed wagging her tail and waiting for me to carry her to the floor.

She scampered to the living room, looking around for her daddy as she did any other morning we fell asleep in bed while Dennis slept in front of the TV. I made our coffee and his toast, and she circled excitedly at the back door while I pulled on my parka and green rubber boots to bring his breakfast to the shop.

I found him in the workshop area, chatting with his two employees. They drifted away when he finished his sentence, and he turned to look quizzically into my eyes, knowing I'd gone to bed upset and wondering what my mood would be. I chose normal.

"Here you are, baby," I said, handing him the mug and offering a kiss. He kissed my lips, pulling back to look deep into my eyes and check my emotional temperature again. I smiled and planted anther kiss on his lips.

"Oh baby, I missed your cuddles last night! I missed being the middle spoon between you and Lulu," he said sweetly, knowing that three of my favourite words from him are *I miss you*. I smiled larger and we kissed some more, melting the uncertainty that was weighing the air between us.

I wanted him to understand that we could have moments, and they could pass into the ether without disrupting the stream of goodness that was growing between us. That we didn't need to interrupt our collective history of non-fighting. That yes, I might get offended sometimes, but I could come back to normal without making him pay for the storm my brain periodically whipped up. That I could make my way past the ruckus and come back to the fact that, hey, sometimes people have blips, but ultimately everything is going to be okay.

I wanted him to know that I'd still love him, and it would show in my actions. That I favoured his peace of mind over fighting, and that I had my own peace of mind well in hand. I wanted him to see that no matter what, he could predict that I'd still care enough about his needs to make him toast and coffee in the morning. That I cared more about him than I did about my ego.

We tend to view intimacy as something that's fleeting, taking place for a moment behind our bedroom doors. But let me redefine intimacy for you, and help you understand that intimacy is much more than the feeling you get when you hold each other close. It's how you handle each other so the current of love continues to flow with little to no interruption. It's how you resolve issues in a way that maintains closeness so they stop creating wedges you need to overcome over and over.

Intimacy is affection, yes. But it's also borne of the confidence we have in each other, in our ability to remain friends no matter what, and in the comfort found in the familiarity and understanding we give each other.

True intimacy happens when your relationship offers you the emotional safety you seek.

CHAPTER 44

Get to the Bottom of It

I'm sure you've seen the play on the word intimacy, "into me see." It's a reminder that in order for real intimacy to flow you have to be able to see, and accept, your partner as a whole. But sometimes we make it hard for someone to see inside us, throwing up walls and smokescreens in defense because we're afraid our true thoughts and feelings will scare people away.

I've been teaching you that it's okay to take down your walls and be seen and that, in fact, doing so will draw your partner in because he'll finally begin to understand that not only are you vulnerable, but you'll let him hold your hand and be your shoulder through tough times.

If you're still feeling that allowing your man to be your pillar when you don't feel strong is too much to ask, consider this little factoid.

Ben Franklin once said, "He that has once done you a kindness will be more ready to do you another than he whom you yourself have obliged." He found that asking someone for a favour actually increased how much they liked him and would be willing to do for him. Why? Because there's always a positive emotional kickback when we do something that generates gratitude from someone, and we associate our resulting warm fuzzy with that person, thus liking them more.

Get it? Asking for help from someone actually gives them an opportunity to feel good about themselves. Win win.

So are you feeling more comfortable talking about your bad day and asking for that much needed hug now? I hope so.

But what about him? How can you get him to take down some of his emotional defenses and let you see a little more clearly what's going on inside his head, giving you opportunities to offer your own shoulder?

If your man is anything like mine you're just going to get peeks from time to time, as men seem to have an ingrained mentality when it comes to emotional vulnerability. In their DNA lies the ability to power past feelings so they can get the job done, whether it's leaving behind their mate and children for the purpose of hunting, killing, and bringing back food, or drawing on great stores of courage in order to protect his family from a dangerous predator. Sadness, disgust, and fear have to take a backseat to ensuring the survival of himself and his DNA.

Men are still like this today, just like us women are still able to detect fine detail better than men because that trait helps us be more observant mothers. So how can we work around this part of their personality?

First, you have to show him you're willing to listen.

Second, you have to be a word nerd.

Like us, men are multi-layered. They neatly hide their thoughts and feelings under layers of defenses thinking each one keeps them safe from interfering with getting up and pounding away at the day or keeps you from getting hurt feelings and lashing out in anger. Our job is to teach them that they can have their feelings with us, and we'll keep them our secret or won't retaliate if it's something we don't necessarily like because they clashed with our ego.

How can we do that? By staying calm, open, and accepting of everything they say.

This is where the words "What else?" come in handy. It's your way of saying, "I accept what you've said, and I'm open for more."

Are you talking about whether or not to change careers, have a kid, move to a new home, or any other hot topic? Ask him what he's concerned about, and when he's done talking ask him, "What else?" and keep asking until he's dug as deep as he can go and comes up blank.

Then ask him what he hopes for, then ask, "What else?" till there's nothing left.

Ask him what his regrets are, and patiently repeat, "What else?"

Ask him what he wants from life, what he feels is missing, and what he loves. Go deeply into each one until he's laid out everything he can find within himself. Don't react to anything, don't respond to anything, don't become defensive or justify anything. This isn't the space for that, this is the space for him to safely communicate what's in his mind and heart. Nothing more.

And when he says, "That's all," believe him. There might be more, but that's all for now.

You can take that information and turn it over in your head, and use some of it to help you become a better partner. But should any of it come back and blow up in his face you'll shut him down because he won't feel safe communicating his thoughts with you.

Long ago I'd made a mental deal with myself when it came to my husband. I'd never make him regret saying whatever he willingly put forth. He might confess something that hurt my feelings, but if I ever threw that back in his face what do you think would happen? I'd never get the truth from him, would I?

Did I take some of the stuff he's told me and rant and rave to my girlfriends about how much it pissed me off? You bet I did. But never to him, because I want to keep the honesty flowing and making it safe to do so is the only way how.

So, first, listen. Listen patiently, listen gently, and listen without responding. Just listen.

Second, become an expert at taking each word and giving it considerable weight. Women, me included, have a tendency to want things said our way. But our way is soooo different from men's. Remember, we use 20,000 words a day versus their 5,000, so while they'll communicate their thoughts and feelings it's not going to come out the way we'd do it. So we have to translate.

"How did you like that play?" we'll ask our girlfriend, and she'll say, "Oh my God, it was so awesome! The costumes were really amazing, and I totally cried when she died."

"How did you like the play?" we'll ask our man, and he'll say, "It was good!"

And for us, that has to be good enough because to ask for more taxes their brains as they try to come up with more words to finally please us. If you're wondering what's one of the most annoying thing men find about us, asking for more words is probably it.

So take what they say and give it the weight it deserves, because we should put as much effort into listening to their words as it took for them to communicate them.

CHAPTER 45

I Still Love You

This is my key to forgiveness phrase. You know those moments, the ones where you're standing at a crossroads. The right fork is letting the moment pass while exercising kindness and forgiveness, and the left fork is continuing on in anger, hurt, and frustration. These are the words that facilitate taking the right fork and avoiding an interruption of flowing love.

Men are forgiving creatures, and they're happy to let moments slide by. And look, neither of us are immune from saying things we wished we hadn't. Finding within us the ability to say "I still love you" instead of staying in our corner mulling over what a dick he is or wondering how you're going to undo what you said gives you both the grace you need to get through those stupid little moments.

We need those words as much as he does. They give us a pass when we say something that was too sharp, too grumpy, or too angry at the moment. Being able to go to him and say "I still love you" gives him an opportunity to forgive us our moments.

Those four words can replace all the ones we would use to explain our thoughtless behaviour when it happens, although we're free to explain away once we've started with that. Why do they belong at the beginning of the conversation instead of at the end? Because they convey right away the full intent of going to him in the first place. That you seek reconciliation, not justification or explanation, and they immediately soften his heart and open his arms, making it much easier to get the love flowing again right away.

"I still love you" is all you say when he's had a stupid moment and said something that offended you, and you choose to appreciate the fact that overall he's a good man instead of hating on that one aspect of him you wish he didn't embody. It's the words you say when he's made a mistake but you'd rather stay focused on the bigger, better picture than spin in mishaps and flaws. None of us are perfect, but what we can perfect is the art of moving past little mistakes. We all make them, leaving little steaming landmines in our wake, but being an emotional leader and showing him how you're going to step over them instead of on them creates a ton of gratitude in his heart.

Don't forget to follow up with a nice, long, warm hug so he understands the sincerity behind your words. It's that hug that tells him without a doubt that you meant what you said, and the oxytocin that's released makes you both feel warm and fuzzy and closer to each other. Remember, forgiveness isn't a feeling, it's a series of actions.

So those times when you're an idiot? Go to him, put your arms around him and say, "I still love you. I'm sorry I was so short with you. I'm feeling hormonal and stressed and my mouth got ahead of me. I love you, baby." Then enjoy his hug, enjoy his words of forgiveness, enjoy the lingering feelings of love that perpetuate from this moment. You deserve every little bit.

CHAPTER 46

When You Don't Know What to Say

Say nothing at all.

Simple, right? Boy, did things begin to change in my relationship when I adopted this philosophy. You get a text and aren't sure what to respond? He says or does something that triggers a negative emotions? Don't say a word until you've taken the time to carefully weigh all your options and have cooled down.

Nothing good comes from speaking before thinking, and nothing good comes from saying something in the heat of the moment.

When I began to do this I found that a lot of things I thought I wanted to say actually faded into the ether if I gave myself time to think before reacting verbally. I stopped caring about how much time passed before I said something and began responding with what really counted. I became more conscious and careful of the words coming out of my mouth, and doing that eliminated a lot of fights between us.

I'm not talking about those moments when you're in the car and making conversation, catching up on what's going on at work and gossiping about people you know. I'm talking about those moments where you feel a sudden flush at his words or actions.

In that space between the flush and your reaction, interject silence. Stop, take a moment to pause and reflect on what you might say. You'll find you'll reject a bunch of options and might even, eventually, run out of words and steam before anything even passes your lips.

And that's a good thing.

It means you didn't complicate anything that could have stayed simple. It means nothing's hanging in the air between you, leaving you stewing or wondering what he's going to do or say now. It means a lot of stuff just floats by.

But for the things that stick in your mind, take your time. Use silence as your buffer while you hash out what's going on in your head. If days go by and you're still spinning over something talk to your girlfriends or a professional like moi and figure it out before you bring it to him.

Don't come to your man confused about an issue, looking for him to clear the fog, because chances are he won't be any better at creating clarity than you are. Your best bet is taking the time to reflect about the problem and coming to a solution that you'll be able to present to him when you finally sit down and put it all on the table.

You know those times when men call us women "crazy?" That's their way of saying we're as confused as they are when it comes to dealing with problems. "Holy crap, I just said this little thing, and the next thing I know she's yelling at me and saying I need to fix it, but I have no idea what she's talking about. She's crazy!" Yes, for a man the word crazy seems to be synonymous with emotional and confused.

Sometimes what's driving us crazy is our own feelings over things we don't need to get worked up about. For example, in our early days together the relationship between my man and his ex drove me crazy. She frequently called and if she got his voicemail never left a message, forcing him to call her back for the smallest things. It drove me nuts and I complained about it, ultimately starting a number of fights.

But I began interjecting silence instead and filled that space with thinking, and because of that I came up with the mantra that helped me through all those times going forward. *I know everything I need to know about them.* I know he's just trying to keep her appeased. I know he no longer wants a relationship with her. I know she's needy.

Was I over reacting, over emotional, overblowing the whole thing? Yes. Were my reactions driving a wedge between us? Yes. Could I deal with the whole situation better? Yes, absolutely.

Have you ever blown something out of proportion? Ladies, let me answer that for you.

You did.

And you will again.

A woman's brain is probably the hardest working piece of software on this planet. Kay, I might be exaggerating a bit, but you get the idea. We multifunction like mad, and there's so much stuff that goes through our brain on a daily basis we literally need more sleep than men to recover. Your brain will go off on a tangent at any given time for any given reason, but while it's hard to keep it from running away from us the way it's prone to doing, we can control how we react to all the different directions our firing neurons will take us on.

And if, after all is said and done, you still can't come up with a solution to a problem? Know that how you approach him to help you resolve it makes all the difference in the world.

Coming to him and saying, "I've got a problem with you," is instantly going to make his testicles crawl into his body. I mean, make him defensive. He's gonna pull up the drawbridge and shutter the windows and set archers along the top of the wall, ready to fire back with every reason why you're wrong. And do you know where you're going to get? Nowhere.

But if, on the other hand, you say to him, "I need your advice on something. Do you have time?" you'll get his full cooperation. He might say, "Not now," which is fine. You can then say, "Okay, can you let me know by the end of the day when would be a good time?" and remind him before bed to help you set aside a time that works for both of you. He'll respect that, and he'll respect you for respecting him.

Or he might turn to you right then, ready and willing to listen to what's on your mind. Use "I feel" statements, instead of "you're making me feel." This keeps him from feeling accused, keeps him listening, and keeps him emotionally plugged into your feelings because his defenses aren't getting in the way. Remember to listen to what he says and give each word the weight it deserves. Do not react defensively if his response fires up your ego. If you don't know what to say, say "Okay, thank you" and hug him and walk away so you can get in some more thinking time. Not everything has to be solved right away, so be patient and be open to the process.

Men value what they understand. They *get* thinking twice before talking. They get calming down and letting things go. If you come to them with a concern and a solution or a request for advice instead of freaking out in the moment, you're going to get a lot farther with them because their brains won't defensively block your behaviour.

So what do you want? Do you want a man who listens to you and carefully weighs what you say? Or do you want a man who'll dismiss you with the words "She's just crazy."

The difference lies in what you approach you take with him. Show him you've got your emotions in hand, and he'll give the problems you put before him the attention they deserve.

CHAPTER 47

Let's Be Fair

Have you ever stopped to weigh how much focus you put on his behaviours versus yours? Have you ever sat down and written out the list of what you expect from him, then written out what you feel he should expect from you? If you did that, what would happen? How much thought have you put into what he needs in this relationship, and how would your paper be graded when you consider how well you meet those needs?

Look, I'm not saying a relationship should be one sided, you servicing him while he ignores your needs. What I'm saying is, balance how much you're focusing on how he's meeting yours with some thought into how much you're meeting his. If you're feeling unsatisfied with how your emotional needs are being met, is it possible he's in the same boat?

There's a trend I frequently see in relationships. Often, one person minimizes their partner's needs while hyper focusing on how well they're satisfying theirs. It doesn't seem fair.

But it's not all your fault. The fact is we're fed common misperceptions about men's emotional depths, and a big one is, "The way to keep a man happy is fuck em' and feed em'." Okay, that's simple, but what else are you considering? Nothing?

Being a behaviourist means I've become an expert at noticing what isn't present as much as what is, and what I don't see in that statement is "F & F em', *and* misinterpret their behaviours and make them pay for it, *and* lash out when our hormones surge, *and* become angry at them because we don't realize our amygdala is firing off from stress or fear, *and* withhold affection because we blame them for all of the above."

Sure, keep the home fires burning. Sure, enjoy a satisfying physical relationship together. But what about their happiness? What about ensuring they have what we ourselves are asking for, too?

Ladies, we are so caught up in our own emotions that we're not seeing the forest for the trees.

We need to Re. Lax.

We need to Re. Group.

We need to Re. Think.

We've been blindly following the blind for way too long. Let's change the rules when it comes to picking a mate and when it comes to how we're going to deal with both him and ourselves in this situation. We want an optimal outcome? Then let's focus on what it takes to achieve that.

Don't you want to be in love with your best friend? So the question is, are you treating him as well as your best girlfriend? Or the samw way you'd want her to treat you? Think about that for a second. Would your girlfriend put you on friend suspension if you gave her as much emotional consideration as you give your partner? If you talked to her the same way? If you demanded more of her than you did of yourself?

Are you being fair?

It's okay to say no. I know I wasn't. I'd come at him with anger and want him to appease me, then tell myself he hadn't done enough to catch up with all the issues in my head and lay more anger on him. I'd withhold affection and tell myself he had to work for it. I kept digging psychological holes for him to crawl out of, then raise the bar, dig the hole deeper, and keep him working because my ego was never satisfied.

I kept having mental conversations about everything he wasn't doing right, then constantly ignoring his efforts and demanding more. I spent a lot of time focusing on my feelings but spent no time considering his. Why would I? Men didn't have feelings, right? Men didn't have needs, suffer depression, feel unhappy, or even cry. They were just walking, eating, fornicating machines with basic functions, and all I knew was *he should be trying harder.*

But I wasn't being there for him. I wasn't asking how he was feeling. I wasn't asking myself how I would feel in his shoes. I was focussing on everything I felt he was doing wrong yet ignoring whether or not he was feeling appreciated or taken care of. Emotionally, I was being completely one sided.

But the fact was, how was he supposed to learn how to be there for me? If what I wanted had never been modeled for him how could he know what to do? I needed to calm myself, recognize he had feelings too, and teach him how both of us could feel emotionally safe in our relationship.

I needed to start being grateful for what he did, because it's what I wanted from him. I needed to talk to him gently, with love, because it's what I wanted. I needed to pay attention to what would register to his mind as love, because it's what I wanted. I needed to forgive the years of transgressions and hurts and begin living in the moment with a clean slate. I needed to heal, I needed to start feeling like we were building a solid foundation, and so did he.

The path we were on needed to take a sharp turn. We both knew this, we both needed this, and someone had to be the hero and take us on a new road.

Ladies, we can be the shaman and the guide. We can initiate the healing in our relationships, all it takes is a step back to regroup, an open mind to see things differently, and a willingness to put healing and love above ego. All it takes is a leader.

And that's you.

CHAPTER 48

Time to Heal

How do you get through years of accumulated muck? How do you lay it out, wipe it clean, and put it all behind you once and for all?

When years of feelings of anger, betrayal, and hurt accumulate it can seem like a monumental task to work through it all and come out the other side. Let me tell you, yes, it's a big job, but it's not impossible when two people are willing to do the work involved.

Couples therapy and attending intense group couples workshops are the perfect starting point for the work you'll need to do. Getting out of your home environment and physically immersing yourselves into healing spaces, where the focus is solely on achieving resolution and unity, is an important first step because it forces you both to surrender to the process and give you those important initial tools for continuing the work at home.

Hubby and I probably wouldn't be here today if we hadn't done both. Couples counselling gave us some valuable gems, and taking two days to do nothing but break down walls and discover communication tools while surrounded by other couples going through similar emotional upheaval was incredibly beneficial. There's something about knowing you're not the only one breaking down and rebuilding that accelerates the process.

One of the things you should be learning on this journey is how to write each other a letter that will bare all once and for all. Why a letter? Because writing gives you an opportunity to get everything out, and subsequently reading that letter creates a space where you can express those words without interruption. It creates a flow of release that helps tremendously.

Healing letters are one of the key strategies we learned to heal those old wounds and start anew with each other.

Agreeing to come together and intensely focus on what's on our minds, to work through the emotions swimming inside us and putting everything on paper so we can read our insights to each other is nothing short of cathartic. Doing this every time we felt a build-up in our relationship eventually cleared the air, till we felt there was nothing left to purge.

It's important to put aside time to do this together. It's also important to not hold back when you do something like this because otherwise it's like you're performing a half poop. Get it all out so you don't end up staying backed up.

There are specific steps to pulling off a successful healing letter session and if you can convince him to do this with you great, but if not then investing in an intensive couple's group therapy weekend is worth the money, because he'll likely feel more secure letting loose in a "safety in numbers" scenario. Plus, the guidance of a good moderator can help push you further than you otherwise would go on your own.

There are five steps that help you ensure this experience is rewarding for both of you.

Step 1 – Set time aside to make it happen. Don't spring something like this on him. Instead, explain what you want to do and let him help you find a good time to get it done. You need his emotional cooperation, and letting him mentally prepare will work in your favour.

Step 2 – You've made your appointment and are now together, ready to launch. Give him a copy of the instructions, and make sure you have a copy too. There's a lot of detail that goes into a healing letter, and each step is important.

Each of you will pick a private space to go write your letters. It's important that you don't fear being walked in on, because you need to focus on the exercise at hand. One of you can choose to go sit outside, so long as you feel that space is private enough to cry as hard as you want. Have closed doors between you, and have your own boxes of Kleenex, along with plenty of paper and a few pens.

When the first person is done writing their letter simply wait in a common area like the living room for the other to join.

Step 3 – You're each going to write two letters. The first is a letter where you purge all your anger, sadness, hurt, hate, longing, forgiveness, and love. The second is a letter you'll write from your partner to yourself. This letter is the response letter, and it helps set your partner up in the right frame of mind to listen openly. I'm going to give you the details of what goes into each letter a little further on.

Step 4 – Come together when you're both done writing. Choose who'll go first or flip a coin.

Each person will read both letters consecutively, beginning with the response letter. Hearing the response letter first paves the way to being able to deal with the content of the healing letter. The person listening should refrain from saying anything until both letters have been read.

Step 5 – Hopefully, when you're heard each other's letters there's no anger, frustration, or justification of behaviours. Ideally. If one of you feel that there are unresolved issues then another healing letter might be in order because not everything has been purged, or this round of healing letter has dredged up some more old stuff. Hubby and I wrote about a half dozen healing letters to each other before we felt we didn't need to anymore.

Regardless, this round needs to be wrapped up with the exchange of a long, loving hug and the words "I love you, everything is going to be okay." You've both been through an emotional wringer, and letting the dust settle for a bit is good. Keep each other's letters and re-read them. Sometimes it's hard to absorb everything, and we often skim over the good stuff and focus on the bad. Go back to the good stuff and read it over and over. Allow yourself to accept the love those pages contain.

Be sure to learn from the negativity they disclose too. Understand that the issues you'll find in those letters have been caused by history, conditioning, and baggage. Those things are temporary, and with time you'll grow and work through them. What you should be anchoring your emotions on is the love, hope, and forgiveness those letters contain. Fortify yourself with that and use it to keep fighting through the years of backed up negativity. It'll take time, but it's worth the effort. Trust me, the space beyond the light at the end of the tunnel is awesome.

Now, here's what you're going to write in your healing and response letters:

What your healing letter should contain

A healing letter is a place to let it all out. Let me repeat that. A healing letter is a place where you let it alllllllll out. Way too often when I coach couples through this process someone holds back, thinking they're saving their partner from feeling hurt or angry and saving themselves from having to face those emotions. What they don't understand is the space within which you share your healing letters is safe because the methodology used soothes emotions and keeps them from becoming overly inflamed.

Holding anything back just means you're still left with junk in your heart and psyche, and you haven't healed as much as you could. This is your loss, and yours alone. You could have used this opportunity to heal and you didn't. So don't hold back no matter how ugly you think something is, no matter how ashamed it makes you feel, no matter how much you think it'll hurt your partner. Holding it in means it's going to continue to haunt you subconsciously and interfere in your relationship. Let it out.

You're going to cycle through a full range of emotions, which is the beautiful part of all this. Feelings tend to take on layers inside of us, and ultimately love and forgiveness get buried under anger and sadness. By going through your emotions layer by layer you're going to dig through your negative ones and find the positive feelings that are buried deep inside you. Bringing those to light will help you heal together.

Your letter contains emotional sections, and each section needs to be thought out and written about until you feel completely drained of stories that pertain to each feeling. Again, don't hold back. If this letter takes two hours to write so be it. This is your time to work through what's inside of you, and you don't know when this opportunity will come again.

Be sure to cry as much as you want. Pound a pillow as much as you want. Hold yourself as much as you want. Stop and emote every time you need to. It's important to allow yourself to physically express your feelings as they come to the surface, so sink deeply into them and give yourself permission to really feel. This process of allowing will let them leave your physical body, and part of this exercise is

5555555

releasing pent up emotions so they stop bubbling up and interfering with the love that should be taking place in your relationship. Feelings aren't esoteric things with no physical presence. Feelings are as real as what your eyes are resting on right now, and you've got to let the negative ones out so you can let the positive ones become your main show.

As you're writing you might find that you create pages and pages of a particular emotion. Don't worry about that, but do be sure you're not spinning out pages for just one story. Instead, keep everything you write brief and to the point. It's enough to write, "I feel so frustrated when you take the car and bring it back with an empty gas tank, and I end up being late to my appointments because I have to add one more thing to do on the way."

For each emotional section you can use these guiding sentence starters to help you dig up and express what's inside you. Use each one till you can't begin a sentence with it anymore, then move on to the next. You might use a particular one a dozen times and then none of the other ones or you may find other ways to begin your sentences for that particular emotion. That's all good; these are just guidelines to help you if you get stuck. Start a new page when you start a new emotion.

Introduction: Dear _____

I'm writing you this letter to express everything that's in my heart. To release all my negative emotions and to give you all the love and positivity you deserve. I'm writing this so we can exchange loving support and move towards a space where all we feel every day are feelings of hope, love, encouragement, and support towards each other. I appreciate your open mind and heart and am grateful for you for taking this moment with me.

(**Anger**) I'm so mad when _____. I get so pissed off when _____. I get really angry when _____. I hate it when _____. I resent you for, when _____. I'm so annoyed when _____. I'm so frustrated when _____. I'm so angry that _____. I feel so bitter about _____. I'm so offended when _____. I'm furious that _____. I start fuming when _____.

(**Sadness**) I'm so sad when _____. I feel sad when I think about _____. It breaks my heart when _____. I cry when I _____. I feel disappointed when _____. I feel lonely when - _____. It hurts when _____. I feel blamed when _____. I wish _____. I feel hopeless when _____. I'm miserable when _____. I feel let down when _____. I'm grieving _____.

(**Fear**) I'm afraid when _____. I'm scared when _____. I'm scared about _____. I'm afraid that _____. I'm afraid you _____. I worry that _____. I feel anxious about _____. I'm nervous that _____. I'm worried you'll _____. I hesitate to _____. I feel insecure about _____.

(**Regret**) I'm sorry I _____. I regret _____.

I'm feel ashamed about _____. I wish I hadn't _____. I should have _____. You deserve _____.

(Forgiveness) I forgive you for _____. I understand that _____. I forgive myself for _____. I'm letting go of _____. I accept and forgive _____.

(Love and Gratitude) I'm grateful for _____. I love you for _____. I love myself for _____. I love us for _____. Thank you for _____. You are _____. I'm so lucky that _____. Together we _____.

What your response letter should contain

Now that you've written your healing letter, it's time to create your response letter.

This is a letter from your partner to you. This letter addresses what you've written in your healing letter and says what you need to hear to feel understood and validated. Think of the words you want to hear from your partner and put it in this letter. This opens their mind to what you need, so be clear and expressive.

"Dear Chantal, I'm so sorry I didn't tell you as much as I should have what I appreciated about you. You deserve to hear those words and knowing how much you need them and withholding them from you hurt your feelings, and I regret doing that. I'm going to try harder to tell you all the positive things that are in my mind about you and our relationship together." And so on.

See what I mean? Write what you need to hear so you can be sure your partner understands. Your response letter is what you're going to read first, and because you've opened the Pandora's Box in such a non-confrontational way your partner is now ready to hear all your emotions without feeling accused and defensive and shutting down. Letting your partner hear what will make you feel loved and accepted first puts them in a loving and accepting frame of mind and creates that safe space to let everything out.

One of the things I often say is, with understanding comes compassion. Open the doors to fully understanding each other and you'll unlock the compassion you need to get you through the transition from hurt and frustration to love and support.

Let him see you cry when you read your letters, and remember that showing your true emotions is how you'll get closer to each other. Intimacy is about brutal reality, so don't be afraid to be so bare, so honest, and so vulnerable that you feel stripped to your core and emotionally drained. Lay it all out, and love each other for the human beings you are. Neither of you are perfect, but you can love each other's perfect imperfections. That's what real intimacy is.

Healing together uncovers a whole new level of love. Now, you're prepared for something deeper. Now, you're set up for the best love you've ever had.

Step 7 – Love

Love is… What you want it to be.

CHAPTER 49

Get Used to Good

When you follow my lead and do the things I've outlined in this book there's a phenomenon that takes place. I had to learn a whole new lesson when I was going through it a while back.

Learning how to say "Yes" to goodness.

You'd think goodness would be something that's easy to adapt to but strangely enough no matter what you experience, whether good or bad, if it's unfamiliar there's going to be an adjustment period.

Ever hear about someone who won millions of dollars in lottery winnings, only to be poor once again within a few years? They couldn't handle living outside their box. They couldn't adjust even if it meant growing into something better than they've ever had.

Sure, a number of them simply continued on being irresponsible or fell prey to unscrupulous people who pounced on the chance to make a quick buck. But for most of them, simmering beneath it all was an inability to get used to the notion that their life could be free of financial struggle forever.

I never knew something like that could happen to me but it did, and I had to learn how to relax and accept when things started to consistently stay amazing in my relationship. Now goodness has become predictable, and our collective psyches are loosening up and relaxing into this amazingness. It's pretty damn cool.

See, once I started to do all the things I've talked about like listening to his pain and apologizing for my part, being predictable when he came home so he didn't get stressed just thinking about walking through the door, meditating to help me deal with my emotions, practicing kindness every day, and saying "I'm sorry" for any transgression no matter the size, we stopped fighting. Completely.

My man became sweeter, kinder, and quickly and readily apologized for his moments of forgetfulness or assholeness. We got good at forgiving each other on the spot and hugging our blips away.

If your experience is similar to mine you're going to go through a period of weirdness, where all will be good but you have an uneasy sense that a shoe is about to drop. Don't worry about this, it's only your brain cycling through its historical patterns and alerting you that theoretically, you're overdue for a fight. Let the moment pass, continue to meditate and shrink your amygdala, and that restless, unsettled, nervous feeling will leave eventually.

Life is spent in cycles, and the best predictor of future behaviour is past behaviour. The more you fill your past with positive experiences together the less your mind will signal that something negative in on the horizon. In the meantime don't succumb to the temptation to pick a fight to validate and alleviate the feeling that you should be upset about something. Relax, release, and create something new now.

Consciously saying yes to goodness is an important step to receiving even more. The opposite of saying yes is rejecting goodness and refusing to acknowledge you deserve it, and because your antennae is always on and attracting your vibe you're creating an uphill battle for yourself. Focus on goodness and take the time to be grateful for it.

Don't set yourself up to fail by rejecting it on a subconscious level. When you sit for your meditation sessions bring up the good things that are happening in your life. Those loving moments you've exchanged with your man, that compliment you got from your boss about your work, the beautiful, sunshiny drive home, how much you laughed when you caught up with a friend, the $15 you won on a scratch and win ticket.

There is so much to be thankful for. Get used to saying thank you and let those words flow from your lips like water over Niagara Falls. I thank my husband all the time for being a good husband, for taking care of me, for making me happy. I have so much to be grateful for because I decided long ago to be grateful for everything, and now I have everything I want.

Like attracts like. What are you thinking about? Focus on what you want, then find where it exists and even if it's tiny, be grateful for it and watch it grow.

You want your man to be more helpful? Then find every little instance where he is and say thank you. A good man will pounce on the opportunity to hear those words more often and will do even more things that make you thankful. You've got to start on a micro level in order to achieve a larger effect.

There are certain words that you can never overuse in a relationship. *Thank you, I'm sorry,* and *I love you for being good* are words that'll never get old. Sprinkle them liberally, and you'll grow deeper and deeper in love while growing into better human beings together.

Hear me on this. Learning how to say yes to goodness is something you have to do. Start here and you'll say yes to goodness when you hit a career benchmark and when good fortune comes your way. You're always choosing anyway, so learn to say yes consciously. Yes to what's amazing and yes to the amazingness that's coming.

I do this little exercise every so often. Whether I'm in the shower, driving in my car, or looking out my bathroom window, I'll feel a surge moment that I surrender to. It's a moving into the future moment, and I feel like I'm about to step into a new reality, if I want. All it requires is a recognition, a decision, a surrender, followed by a Yes God. Yes, I accept. Yes, goodness. Yes, thank you.

I believe these are the moments your life changes. These are the moment that begin to stitch together your future, drawing in life circumstances and people like thread draws together fabric that eventually becomes clothing.

Learning how to say yes to goodness is the most crucial step of all, because without the yes there's only no.

See, I realized a while back that what you feel you deserve and what you'll accept on a spiritual level is what you'll receive.

So I decided right then I would always choose *God, yes*, and ever since my life has been filled with fortune. Hubby and I moved to my dream property, and we've been remarkably peaceful and loving. In one year I wrote three more books, got a radio gig, and had my advice published on Huffington Post. I've given workshops to 80 women, sat on the same stage recently occupied by Tony Robbins to deliver a talk about love, and seen women line up to buy my books.

And I did a lot of God yessing all along the way.

I breathe in moments where my life moves forward. And then I say, feel, cry even, a thank you so deep it feels universal. See? I'm crying right now.

I surrender.

I accept.

God yes.

Thank you.

Dear reader, come with me, it's so awesome when goodness reigns. Let's start a revolution, and together we'll change the landscape of relationships for generations to come. Your kids are going to see what the word harmony means in a loving union and in one's personal life, and they'll learn the best lesson of all from you – that love exists and it's beautiful and it spreads out from inside and infects everything with goodness.

Yes!

CHAPTER 50

Love Is a Verb

Just like forgiveness is a series of behaviours, so is love.

Love is what you do for your partner. It's letting that sharp comment go without saying the negative words buzzing in your head, or it's saying "I'm sorry" for voicing them. It's a stash of Oh Henry! bars for those days when he needs a smile. It's cleaning up what's in his line of sight so he feels like he's come home to a cozy house. It's knowing his love language and ensuring you're speaking it to his heart.

It's forgiving him right away when he says he's sorry and not holding grudges. It's showing gratitude for everything he does and never minimizing his efforts. It's in the effort you put into meditating enough to keep your mind calm, and it's the times you turn to him, seeking comfort, letting him know just how to make you feel better in the moment.

Your devotion to generating love is what'll grow it beyond anything you've experienced or could even imagine. Love is the friendship you have with your partner. It's the respect you show for his feelings. It's the tender strength you offer when he's hit by life and need a soft place to regroup. It's the allegiance you form together to fight by each other's side no matter what, and it's the devotion you show to your collective wellbeing.

Love is all the things you do, no matter how big or small, to consciously make yourself and your partner happy. See, love isn't just about how you feel towards each other; love is all about what you do to make space for love.

Your ego might be saying you should be on the receiving end of loving actions first, but the Mexican standoff that creates blocks the flow of love, and you ultimately end up feeling like you're not getting enough. If you unlock love and start giving it freely it's going to flow right back at you, and you're going to feel like you've got all the love in the world right in the palm of your hand.

And finally, love is the ruby red shoes Dorothy wore in The Wizard of Oz. Don't think love is something that's "out there." No no no. Love is something you've been wearing all along, and it's just waiting for you to notice that the power is yours and yours alone to make all your wishes come true.

So unlock the power of love. Don't worry, everything is going to be okay.

Afterword

Relationships. Like the weather, they are sometimes sunny, calm, and punctuated by beautiful sunsets and sunrises. But at times they become wild and stormy, and it's in these moments that you must batten down the hatches and hunker down, hoping you've effectively protected yourself from torrential rain and blowing debris.

But every storm passes, as per the law of nature. And hopefully, when all is said and done, you'll realize how much the rain and wind benefited your parched crops and shook dead limbs off your trees, helping you move forward in life fueled and renewed.

Learning how to appreciate and grow through the toughest storm is the most important quality you'll develop. Lean into the storms, seek the lessons they provide, and teach others the tools you learn as you leave the old you behind and grow into someone better.

I remember a segment on CBC Radio about the glut of painkillers in today's society, and I admired a woman with a back injury who avoided drugs that would dull her pain and keep her from knowing what her body needed to heal. We should all strive to lean into pain so we can learn how to improve ourselves, instead of avoiding life's issues.

Growth is rarely a comfortable process, but after each spurt there are moments of joy and gratitude. So welcome pain, because once you work through it you reap the benefits of an upgraded life. Become a teaching tool, and the benefits will increase tenfold, as your heart is forced to grow even bigger to contain the happiness you feel knowing you've helped someone become happier too. It's a wonderful cycle.

Value your capabilities and how they contribute to love. Be loving and generous with your partner, and practice having a peaceful mind. This gives them space to change as well, and when two people feel awesome magic is created. If you become a master of growth and your partner continues to value dysfunction at least you've learned what it takes to have everything you need in a relationship, freeing you to move forward and find the ultimate companion.

I wish you all the patience, understanding, and love you need to get through your tough times. You deserve the amazing moments developing your brain for growth supplies you with. Give yourself a chance to get through the discomfort with a clear mind, and you'll find something beyond what you could imagine on the other side. I did, and I'm here, waiting for you.

Come, my sister.

About The Author

CHANTAL LIVES IN ONTARIO, Canada with her husband Dennis and two dogs, Maggie and Lulu. She is a Human Relations and behavioural expert with a successful practice, helping clients learn how to find and keep a "magical" loving relationship. As a public speaker, workshop leader, private coach, writer, and frequent media contributor, Chantal is busy distributing advice far and wide in the hopes of creating loving unions that will resonate for generations. Chantal is also a member of Zonta, a UN recognized international organization of professional women working together to advance the status of women worldwide through service and advocacy.

Visit Chantal Heide at
www.CanadasDatingCoach.com
You Tube – Chantal Heide
Instagram - @canadasdatingcoach
Twitter - @CanDatingCoach
Facebook – Chantal Heide, Canada's Dating Coach
Podbean and Itunes – Chantal Heide

References

Step 1

1. http://www.telegraph.co.uk/news/10574941/Women-far-more-likely-than-men-to-seek-counselling-for-anxiety.html

2. http://elitedaily.com/dating/guys-more-emotional-girls/1077730/

3. http://www.castanet.net/news/Natural-Health-News/63064/Negative-effects-of-Cortisol

4. http://www.livestrong.com/article/203790-what-happens-during-an-adrenaline-rush/

5. http://news.harvard.edu/gazette/story/2011/01/eight-weeks-to-a-better-brain/

Notes

_____

_____

_____

_____

_____

_____

_____

_____

_____

_____

_____

_____

_____

_____

_____

Notes

Notes

Made in the USA
Las Vegas, NV
14 April 2021